A WINDOW

INTO

EASTWOOD WRITERS'

GROUP

British Library Cataloguing in Publication Data.

Names, characters and incidents in this book are products of the authors' imaginations or are used fictionally.

Edited and copy design by Angela Rigley
Cover design by Annette Jones

Published by Eastwood Writers' Group.
www.eastwoodwritersgroup.com

CONTENTS

INTRODUCTION

A Window into Eastwood Writers' Group is an anthology, a collection, a garland, of our work. We are a diverse group who share a love of writing. We have produced this book to showcase our work, and encourage ourselves and others to keep writing and improving. Some of our poems and stories will make you smile, others may make you cry, and maybe a few will produce the retort: "I never thought of that".

Some of us are published authors, others are trying to become published, but we all love to write. We hope you enjoy reading our book and that it encourages you to try letters, novels, diaries or anything more than a shopping list.

We are based near Eastwood, Nottinghamshire, the home of D H Lawrence, and one day some of us may be known as well as he. The rest of us will write at home and meet every Tuesday at Brinsley Parish Hall to critique our efforts.

Dianne Rasmussen
Chairman of Eastwood Writers Group 2014

A 'chairman' is not necessarily a man any more than a catastrophe is always caused by a cat, although both can be.

BACK TO WORK

Ann Cooper

I'm full of guilt; you see the reason
is I've lazed away the summer season.
So, this morning I decided I must write
a masterpiece, something clever, erudite.
Upstairs eagerly I went to set the scene,
switched on the computer, faced the empty screen.
Two hours later, drenched in perspiration,
admitted defeat—no bloody inspiration!

WANTING YOU

Barrie J Kinsella

Immaculate in purple vestments,
Never varying in neatness,
My eyes feasting as ever
In silent wanting.
Many years have passed
Since we were first introduced;
The courtship between you and me
Goes relentlessly on through time.
Sometimes I am strong, months go by
Before I seek you out,
To hold and devour you;
Often I am weak; to see you
Every day is my aim.
Is there to be no end
To this one-sided adoration?
You are sweetness itself to me,
But, alas, my nemesis;
Will I ever be released
From your thrall,
And regain my youthful figure
By refusing to brush my lips
On you, my weight-inducing chocolate bar?

WORMS

Dianne Rasmussen

"Nobody loves me, everybody hates me,
I think I'll go and eat worms.
Long, thin, slimy ones that slip down easily
And short, fat, juicy ones that stick."

"That's a funny poem," John said, "especially to recite to a cat."

Jane stroked the white and black cat's head. "I'm just preparing her for the worm tablet she needs to take."

"Worm tablet? I thought cats ate meat and fish, or is this one of your money-saving schemes?"

"Ha, ha, very funny, but you won't be laughing when you've had to help me give one to all four of them."

He smiled. "That shouldn't be difficult."

Jane opened her mouth as if to say something but closed it again before smiling briefly and saying, "We'll see."

"Right, we'll start after breakfast."

Later that morning Jane carried a towel and a packet of tablets into the lounge. "Are you ready, John?"

"Ready? Ah, yes." He put down his paper and looked wonderingly at the towel. "What's that for? Do you have to wash their paws before you do it?"

She laughed. "I'd like to see you try. Now, do you want to administer the tablet or hold the cat? I think we'll start with Tiggie, she'll be the easiest.

"Right." John went to the chair with the red cushion and picked up the tabby cat sitting there. "Time for your worm tablet, Tigg." He sat her on his knee, gave her a few strokes then put out one hand. "Where's the tablet?"

"Aren't you going to wrap her in the towel?"

"We don't need a towel, do we Tigg? Just give me a

pill and I'll give it to her."

Jane counted them before picking one out.

"Why are you counting them?"

"They came in a pack, and I'm just checking we have a spare, in case anything goes wrong."

"Oh, ye of little faith," he said as he wrapped his arm around Tiggie, forced her mouth open and popped in the pill.

Jane was impressed, but smiled when he let go of the cat and the pill slid from the corner of her mouth onto his trouser leg. It was hard not to laugh as she wrapped the towel around the tabby body that had been about to slink out the door. But Tiggie was determined not to be wrapped up and, after much squirming, she jumped onto the floor and straight under the chair.

Jane lay down and spoke gently to her for a few moments, but then stood up. "I think we'll have to leave it for now. She's not going to cooperate, and forcing will just frighten her."

"Mmm. There must be a simpler way of getting a cat to take a tablet. I'll think about it." He bent down and spoke to her. "You're let off for now but I'll have you later."

Jane passed down a cat sweet. "Give her this to show there are no hard feelings."

Tiggie was very suspicious but her sense of smell reassured her and, after several seconds thinking, she devoured the treat.

"Now that gives me an idea," John announced. "If I put the tablet in her food then she'll eat it without realising."

"Well, you can try." Jane remembered her many attempts in the past to fool cats into taking medication. "You have to remember that cats have an excellent sense of smell. She'll be able to detect the offending tablet and, even if she eats the food, you'll find the pill left neatly on the side of the plate."

His face screwed up with concentration. "Perhaps we can crush the tablet and mix it with a smelly food like sardines."

"It's possible, but sardines aren't strong enough. Also, you have to make sure the cat eats every last scrap of the food, otherwise the de-worming may not work. With four cats to treat we would have to isolate each one to be sure they were not eating each other's."

John's face acquired a look of defeat. "So, how do we get the wormers down them? Other people with cats must have this problem."

"Yes, which is why I brought a towel. If one of us holds the cat firmly, making sure they can't get their paws out, the other person can open its mouth, pop the pill in, then hold it shut, whilst stroking the throat to make it swallow."

"That works, does it?"

"It does, usually, though there are no guarantees. You just have to try your best and accept that you may lose the odd pill, which is why I always buy at least one more than I need."

"Okay, let's have another go, shall we?" John said.

"We could try with Prince, but Tiggie is too spooked to do it now, and the other two know something's going on and have disappeared."

It took three days to administer all the de-worming tablets. Two boxes of treats were used to reward the cats when they had swallowed their expensive medicine.

John stroked the last one's head with relief. "Thank goodness that's all done. Presumably, we'll have to do it again next year?"

"Actually, the instructions say they work for three months," Jane said, watching the look of horror creep over his face. “But I only administer them when I have evidence that one of them has worms, and that’s not very often.”

John looked relieved, and two cats looked up, asking for more sweets.

POEMOTH

Annette Jones

I was woken in the night
by a poem, fluttering like a moth
round my head, insistent,
but like a moth of rare beauty
to a lepidopterist.

Switching on the light
to keep it close, I attempted
to pin it with my pencil
to the page.

This morning I get to see
if I caught it, my precious specimen,
marvellous, multicoloured, mythical, megamoth!
Or if it got away.

Or worse,
If it was in fact nothing
but a common, brown, speckled,
ordinary moth.

THE SUN-KISSED PASSAGES

Mike Hemstock

The sun-kissed passages of life
Run quickly through the hourglass of time.
The dunes are formed by the winds of change,
As the ups and downs of life itself are formed
And move onto Autumnal phases
Where dreams become golden and mellow
As years go by.

Unless we care, 'Earth' will be blown away,
As the sands of time are blown away.

THE BIKE

Alfred J Holt

This is a story you will find hard to believe. Nevertheless, it is true, and unprovoked. It is about me, my beautiful brand new Dawes hand-made, blue racing cycle, and a stream of hot rays from the heavens on a fine Sunday morning. The bike and I had an experience…

Bloody potholes! The sun in my eyes prevented me from missing a wide crack in the tarmac. The front wheel went down and I flew over the handlebars, and landed on my forehead—I didn't wear a helmet; I couldn't see the point.

Blood streamed down my face and into my mouth. I couldn't get up, for my left leg was distorted and tangled with the bike.

Not a solitary soul in sight. Ranmore Common was not generally occupied early on a Sunday morning.

Then, in the rays of sunlight, I saw figures clambering over me, whilst others of the same height—about twelve inches tall—were taking a great interest in the bike. They had gold-coloured sticks in their hands, and were tapping the smashed-up frame and bent front wheel.

I must have passed out but, as I did so, I remember a little figure blowing into my ear.

I awoke with a start and sat bolt upright. Wow, what a dream. But had it been a dream? I had my pyjamas on, and my clothes were neatly folded on the side, next to my bed, so I had definitely been asleep.

I went downstairs and asked my mum and dad what time I had come home. Well after they had gone to bed, apparently, probably in the early hours. I looked in the hall mirror: no dried blood, no gash in my head. Then I hurried to the shed to view my bike. Yep, it was there, proud and shining in the morning light, looking clean and highly polished. Just as I turned away I did a double take. Something was poking out from the saddle.

I pulled out what can only be described as a golden stick, about six inches long.

SPRING IS SPRUNG

Angela Rigley

Foxes peeking, lurking, seeking
dinner for their young;
Rabbits nibbling, hares a-wriggling,
eager for a run;
Lambs a-leaping, shepherds keeping
careful watch for danger;
Ewes a-munching, rams all bunching;
Can they sense a stranger?
Blackbirds squawking, magpies talking;
have they heard it too?
Jays a-flashing, herons dashing
in the misty hue;
Buzzards soaring, eagles roaring;
surely they can see?
Starlings wheeling, jackdaws dealing;
What's that in the tree?
Crows a-cawing, mice a-gnawing
in their nests below,
Deer a-prancing, fawns a-dancing,
too happy to stay low,
Buds unfurling, leaves uncurling,
opening to the sun;
Nature's mantle is unfolding;
What joy now spring is sprung.

A DISH SERVED COLD

Nell

Cross opened the door, stared at the thing on the doorstep and promptly closed it again. He stomped off to the phone and called the local police. Sergeant Brown would have to do something this time.

'I'm sorry, Mr. Cross. But there's nothing I can do. No crime has been committed; far from being a theft, there has been an addition.' The policeman sounded tired and just about to lose his temper.

'But what about trespass? They must have come onto my land to leave the thing. I bet it was that Wright from next door; he'd do anything to win.'

'I've just put the phone down from speaking to Mr. Wright,' said Sergeant Brown. 'He's also having problems. Someone has left a large planter containing african marigolds, surrounded by eke… ecu… things that look like house leeks, on his front garden. He was sure it was you.'

'Echevaria,' said Cross helpfully, 'and it wasn't me; that's parks and gardens stuff. They might still plant them in Torquay and Bournemouth, but nobody uses them much now. What are you going to do about these gnomes?'

'As I said, Mr. Cross, no real crime has been committed. Nobody has reported the theft of said objects, so it's not just kids larking about, especially since the arrival of the planter next door, and as for trespass, again, we can't do anything. It really boils down to a crime against good taste, and if we could do anything about that, half the town planners in England would be behind bars.'

Cross slammed down the phone. Good taste indeed! Didn't the man realise the judges were due that week? And gnomes were definitely not part of his scheme. The annual Best Kept Garden Competition was his focus in life, as it was for Wright.

Honours were currently even; he had won last year, and Wright the year before. It really depended who was judging. His front garden was a tasteful arrangement of mainly foliage plants and shrubs and, fortunately, the judging took place just as his acers and hostas were at their prime.

Wright's garden was a shrine to Vita Sackville-West. Cross could remember the day he'd returned from Sissinghurst and ripped out the entire arrangement of lawn and roses. He'd watched the deliveries arrive: the weeping pear—pyrus salicifolia—if he was not mistaken, the box hedging, and a garden centre full of white-flowered perennials. He had to admit that the result was good, not original, but good. Wright certainly knew his plants, and the way that pyrus peeped over his yew certainly added to his own patch.

Cross sighed. Better move that bloody gnome. He had three of the things now, one fishing, one playing cricket and the latest leaning on a spade. Someone really had it in for him, but who? There was no one else in the town even close to the standards of Manton Avenue, and whoever it was certainly knew how to hurt; gnomes for him and tasteless parks and gardens for Wright.

He humped the gnome round to the back garden shed and put it out of sight with its friends. They winked up at him in a cheery, brightly-coloured way as he closed and locked the door. He reeled out his hose and his snail-hunting spike and went to work.

He spent a contented hour among the hostas. No snail or slug that valued its life would dare go near; those that did, lured by the prospect of a free meal, were swiftly speared. It was a time-consuming way of dealing with the little blighters, but worth it—no bright blue pellets for his garden. As he straightened up, he could hear the rhythmic click of Wright's shears as he trimmed his box hedges. Normally, he would ignore his neighbour, even if they came face to face, but desperate times called for desperate measures.

'Evening, Wright,' he called. 'I hear you're having a spot of bother, too.'

'You're not joking,' replied Wright. 'African marigolds, I ask you. What if the judges had seen them? And I've just discovered a pot of bright purple petunias pushed in the front. Must be a phantom park keeper. How's your reclining nude?'

'My what!' gasped Cross.

'That gnome near the front, underneath the acer palmatum.'

Sure enough, there she was, coyly facing the street, a reclining, nude gnome with a distinctly come-hither expression. Cross struggled to get to her, without crushing the heuchera.

'Have you got a moment, Wright?' he called. 'They must have shoved her in with a pole. If you could give a push from your side, I might just be able to reach her.' The prongs of a fork came into view as Wright manoeuvred the offending gnome within reach.

'That better?'

'Thanks,' gasped Cross, lugging the concrete temptress out, whilst trying to find a suitable hand hold which didn't involve unseemly portions of her anatomy. 'Fancy a beer? I have a couple of bottles in the fridge.'

Adversity had done what nothing else could. Wright appeared on Cross's drive and the two rivals shook hands. Beer in hand, they sat in Cross's back garden, enjoying the last of the evening sun.

'Who could be doing this?' mused Cross. 'Hasn't Gloria seen anything?' Cross was a widower, as was Wright. They had both lost their wives within eighteen months, but whilst Cross had settled into the single life without problem, Wright had become friendly with Gloria, a younger widow from the Gardening Club. She had promptly moved in and insisted on introducing him as her "Significant Other".

'Gloria's left,' said Wright. 'I came home three weeks ago and found a note and a solicitor's letter. She said I thought more of my garden and our rivalry than I did of her. Her solicitor said I should donate half my possessions to the bitch.'

'You're not selling up?' said Cross, surprised at the depth of indignation he felt on his rival's behalf.

'No chance. My solicitor pointed out that it was my house and she had no claim. Haven't heard a thing since. I've no idea where she is even; good riddance.'

'It couldn't be her, could it? You know, leaving all these gnomes and that?'

'No chance, she couldn't plant up like that. I think she only joined the Club in search of men.'

Wright seems to have come to his senses at last, thought Cross. Anyone could see all she had wanted was a meal ticket.

They parted more amicably than they would have believed possible, agreeing to attend the prize giving together.

Thus, three days later, they stood nervously in the Town Hall, being bored to death by the Mayor's speech.

‘Can’t he say a sentence without a cliché?’ whispered Wright.

‘I think it’s in his job description,’ murmured Cross. ‘Come on, man, get on with it.’

‘And now,’ proclaimed the Mayor, ‘what you’ve all been waiting for, the results of the Ovington Best Kept Garden Competition. The judges toured the town anonymously as usual and, as usual, they had a very difficult job. Taking everything into consideration, and bearing in mind the very tricky growing conditions this spring, the results are as follows:’

‘Get on with it,’ muttered both Cross and Wright.

‘In joint second place, both highly commended, are Mr. Wright and Mr. Cross. The judges felt that two outstanding schemes, both showing a high level of horticultural knowledge and expertise, were let down by some inappropriate planting and garden ornaments. Sorry, gentlemen, I didn’t quite catch that?’

Both Wright and Cross had let fly different, but equally profane comments.

‘This year our winner is Mr. Palfrey of 15 Preston Close. Would he join me here, on the rostrum, to receive his trophy?’

‘It’s that little Hitler of a planning officer,’ exclaimed Cross. ‘You remember, the one who wouldn’t let me extend my garage!’

‘Never mind that,’ growled Wright, ‘look who’s with him’.

With a smug expression on her face, and her arm firmly through Palfrey’s, Gloria advanced towards the Mayor. As she passed the two nonplussed men, she gave an almost imperceptible wink, reminding Cross forcibly of the nude gnome.

‘I’ll bet he got those echevaria from the Parks Department,’ said Wright, echoing Cross’s thoughts, ‘and I reckon she put him up to it.’

The rivals wandered home, making a short diversion to look at the winning garden.

‘It’s a good lawn,’ said Cross.

‘But not a patch on ours for design and planting,’ sighed Wright. ‘“Highly Commended”. It’s an insult.’

The next spring, preparations were again made for the competition. Cross and Wright put in even more effort than usual, but were co-operating, particularly on security.

One evening, whilst sitting with a beer in Wright’s garden, Cross spoke up. ‘I’ve walked past that Palfrey’s garden today. I think he’s going for it again this year. His lawn’s looking really good.’

‘Takes more than a bit of grass,’ said Wright.

‘I’ve been thinking. We could always go for a bit of tit for tat,’ mused Cross, assessing his friend’s reaction carefully.

Three weeks later, Cross and Wright were declared joint winners of the contest. They had particularly enjoyed the part of the Mayor’s speech outlining why the previous year’s winner had been disqualified.

‘The judges were astounded to see, picked out in darker grass, the words “Bugger Off”. This is not the type of display the town wants and the Council’s solicitor has been asked to investigate possible legal redress.’

Cross had a job to keep a straight face. He and Wright had enjoyed mixing up the extra-strength lawn feed in the bottle and watching the words appear, as the treated grass greened up over the following five days, just in time for the judging. Palfrey alternately stuttered apologies and disclaimed responsibility.

Gloria was keeping quiet. The handwriting had looked awfully familiar.

LIFE CONTINUES

Gordon F Butler

The church, cool, quiet, peaceful,
the lily-crowned coffin, focus of attention;
a few people, some kneel in prayer,
others sit, waiting, heads bowed.
More arrivals,
footsteps hushed by carpeted floor,
voices hushed by custom.

Tail-coated undertaker
ushers the family to the front.
They sit; silence;
a bell rings; all stand.
The priest enters, the choir sings,
the Mass has begun.
"We are gathered here today
to give thanks for the life of …."

Memory fills out the picture:
playing cards in the club,
smiling, laughing, cursing;
talk of horses, politics, football
and, occasionally, even work.

Now called from life, no warning given,
too soon for those left behind,
wife, children, brothers, sisters,
nephews, nieces, grandchildren.
The rites of passage necessary for all;
the last goodbye, just for now, we believe.

The offertory procession:
two of the grandchildren bring the gifts.
As they pass, sixty years roll back.
The boy, eight years old,
the hair, the build, the walk,
the man who is at rest
walks once more up the aisle.
His heritage lives on.

BIG FAT JOHN

Tony Butler

He stood five-foot-six, weighed eight-forty-five,
kind of wide at the shoulder, and broad at the hip,
and every one knew
you didn't cut down the chips
for Big John,
Big Fat John.

It happened one summer in the shopping mall,
in the local drive-through burger bar;
well, he always drove through,
'cos he couldn't walk far,
Big John,
Big Fat John.

He asked for, "Six burgers with a bucket of fries,
six cokes, three shakes, and a lemonade,
and give my regards
to the PC Brigade."
Big John,
Big Fat John.

They sent him spring water and a salad instead,
said they were only thinking of him,
and how handsome he'd be
when he was slim,
Big John,
Big Fat John.

Well, just about as mad as a man could be,
John clambered out of his automobile,
made the shockers groan,
and the metal squeal,
Big John,
Big Fat John.

'Ban Fatty Foods' it said on their shirts.
Big John turned his back and bent down low,
then he let rip
a mighty rear end blow,
Big John,
Big Fat John.

Gassed, the PC Brigade fell down to the floor.
Now the other customers gave a mighty cheer,
and they bought Big John
a gallon of beer,
Big John,
Big Fat John.

Fifty years later and they're all long gone,
except for big John, now ninety-six;
got no hair or teeth
but he sucks on crisps,
Big John,
Big Thin John.

SIX FEET UNDER

David Brailsford

Hello.

My name is Freddie and, when I was alive, I earned my living playing Pantomime Dames between 1810 and 1818. Unfortunately, I died on stage at the height of my career.

Yes! I literally died on stage, right in the middle of a performance as Widow Twanky in Alladin.

You can find me in the cemetery, where you will see me, most nights, sitting on top of my grave stone, rehearsing my lines.

The following tale unfolded here:

Rain had been falling heavily all day, so I was glad to be out of my wet hole. As I sat, pondering on my past theatrical glory, I noticed, but a few yards away, a newly-dug grave.

It seemed the grave-digger had toiled all day in the pouring rain, taking care to ensure that the hole was exactly six feet long, three feet wide and a good six feet deep, an excellent feat, to prevent the saturated soil from collapsing on itself. He must have been very proud of his workmanship.

At the haunting hour I heard a sudden commotion as the rusty iron gates creaked open, and a man staggered in my direction, singing a raucous, ribald song. He must have downed a belly-full of ale in the local hostelry that night, for he weaved his way, stumbling from tombstone to tombstone, cursing profusely.

WHOOPS.

With a sickening thud, he fell into the newly-dug grave and lay prostrate for some time.

He groaned, rolled over onto his back, and his eyes opened to the darkness around him. Peering upwards, he saw the outline of the hole above.

His torpid mind cleared, as he began to rapidly sober up… Well, wouldn't yours?

Leaping to his feet, he cried out, "God Almighty, I'm in a grave." With a banshee-like wail, he flung himself upwards towards the lip of the hole, grasping wildly for a grip, but all he found was wet, yielding soil that fell down onto him as he tumbled back.

"Lord, help me," he gurgled, as fear grasped his throat.

Time and time again, he sprang to the skies, but always with the same result, until he lay sobbing, covered from head to foot with clingy, wet soil.

As suddenly as it came, his terror broke, for he saw himself, a sweating mass, crouching pitifully at the bottom of this nightmare, so his mind began to reason:

If I carry on, like this, I'll bury myself.

Crying for help was to no avail, so he felt for the safest spot, slumped down, to await cock crow, and for people to walk past the cemetery, and fell asleep.

An hour passed and, lo and behold, another drunk must have made the decision to take the short cut home. He crashed into the grave, not noticing the first drunkard. Then, realising where he was, hysterically screaming for God to help him, he scrambled, sobbing and pleading for rescue, and shaking in abject fear.

The first man thought, *If he carries on like this he'll have a heart attack.* Then, laboriously rising to his feet, he silently approached his new companion and, gently touching him on the back, he whispered, "You won't get out like that."

BUT HE DID.

WHINGEING WASHING MACHINES

Shirley McIntyre

Oh, well, I don't suppose you owe me anything, but for goodness sake, you choose your moments. Here I am, with umpteen bags of stinky washing, after two weeks in the caravan, everything soggy with sand, sweat, and tears. And you, my reliable Indesit, decide to rebel.

I'm the first to admit you've been a strong workhorse, through thick and thin, winters and summers, but did you have to choose now, the rainiest month for a zillion years, to start bemoaning your lot?

It was the ominous clickety click with every spin that made me suspect something was horribly wrong. After unloading sheets, t-shirts and underwear from your 'Hot Wash—for really stubborn stains' programme, I saw it, just peeking through one of the holes in your stainless steel drum. Talk about heart-sink time! With great trepidation I pulled it out, certain it must be one of your vital organs, or a mysterious Indesit innard, at the very least.

At that moment my other half appeared.

"What do you reckon this is, dear?"

He took it, held it up to the light, and said, "It's come out of one of your bras; one of those wire thingamajigs."

"Never!" I peered down to my chest. "My boobs aren't that big!"

I rummaged through the freshly-washed whites, and there it was, my very expensive 'Ann Summers, Touch-Boost, Multiway, Deep Plunge 36D', looking sadly lopsided.

So...a million thanks my dear, old, loyal Indesit. If you hadn't alerted me to that random, rogue, underwire, rattling in your drum, I would have looked a right TIT in that tight-fitting dress I wore for the party later. Sadly lopsided, in fact...

There was once a voluptuous scribe
Whose booby drooped down at one side.
Then somebody told her,
She'd ‘bust’ her boulder-holder.
Shirl had wanted to curl up and die!

TEA WITH GRANDMA

Chrissie Lloyd

I loved my visits to Grandma Sharpe's bungalow. She was my mum's mother.

I had considered her to be a chubby lady, until one day 1 saw her undress. I counted seven layers of clothes: a woolly cardigan over a woolly jumper, thick cotton blouse, a petticoat, a boned, uncomfortable-looking bodice, and a cotton vest, with brassiere beneath. Then I realised she was skinny.

Tea at Grandma's was a wonderful event. Her bone china tea service held mouth-watering treats: plates piled high with just-made bread and cakes, boiled ham, still warm, freshly-picked tomatoes, lettuce and radishes, and home-made chutney. Sherry trifle was my first taste of alcohol—Grandma didn't skimp on the sherry.

The bone china teapot was filled with steaming hot tea, made with loose tea leaves (tea-bags hadn't been invented). Our cups would be filled with Grandma's special brew. I'd drink mine quickly.

"I've finished my drink, Grandma."

"Patience," she would say, "wait for everyone else."

I knew the routine off by heart: swirl my cup anti-clock-wise three times, then turn the cup upside-down on my saucer, and sit patiently.

Because I was the youngest I'd be left 'til last to gain Grandma's attention. Then I'd sit transfixed while she scrutinised the inside of my cup. Those tea-leaves were my future, and she translated. She would see initials of people I'd meet, and whether they'd be tall or little, fair or dark. Any forthcoming journey would be there, either long or short, and we'd see if it would be by car, bus, train or air.

She knew when I'd receive a parcel or letter, all my future achievements, and if someone was jealous or proud of me.

I believed everything Grandma said, although I never really checked if they came true. I enjoyed my visits any day but Sunday, as on the 'Sabbath' Grandma refused to 'Read the Cups'.

Sometimes I spent the school holidays at her bungalow, with no bathroom, just a cold tin bath, unhooked from the wall outside. The toilet was outside in a type of shed, an add-on to the main building, not flushed by water, just emptied when it became full, and the contents buried in a hole, dug in the garden. Dad said it made good rhubarb, but I wasn't sure what he meant.

In the copse alongside her home there were fun places to play with the local children with whom I made friends.

I loved my Grandma Sharpe, with her rosy cheeks, and a face I thought resembled a peach. She smelled of a floral cologne, mint or blackberries, not like my friend's granny who smelled of mothballs.

Grandma was always busy. She would cut up her old cotton and woollen clothes into two-by-five inch strips, and make floor mats by pegging them to some sacking. Her vegetables and fruit pies contained freshly-picked produce from her garden. Thus her kitchen smelled deliciously aromatic.

My Grandma Sharpe never saw a computer or mobile phone. Everyone corresponded by writing letters, posted in a public mail box. I imagine that when my grandchildren are grandparents, their grandchildren won't know what a public mailbox is, now that texting and e-mails have taken over.

I know my grandchildren laugh at my computer skills being non-existent, and I'm the only person they know who types on a typewriter and, when they too have grandchildren, no doubt there will be more things that become out-dated.

I don't think I resemble Grandma, apart from liking to recycle, but my favourite memory of her will always be at teatime, when she would read the tea-leaves.

THE PRESENTATION

Dawn Raffle

The Managing Director, his face wreathed with smiles, patted Derek on his back. The biggest account in the advertising business had just passed back to our agency after five years, and all eyes were on the man who had brought it home: Derek Townsend, the seducer, the lover, the rat.

Seeing him revelling in the applause and congratulations made me feel sick. I gripped my glass of champagne and silently repeated to myself, 'Ellen, grin and bear it.'

Drinking a toast to the toe rag was too much, so I quietly slipped away from the boardroom, back to the office, hoping to avoid the humiliation of the staff seeing me in tears. However, my respite was short. I could hear voices coming near and was fumbling in my bag for a tissue, when a man's voice said, "Here, use this."

The embarrassment at being discovered crying trebled when I recognised my consoler was none other than Mr Bennet, the Office Manager. Automatically, I accepted the tissue he offered. He looked around at the group of people approaching and said, "I think different surroundings might be appropriate. I need to talk to you." He nodded towards a few of the staff who were casting curious looks in my direction. The office was open plan, and I was thankful to be ushered outside, to escape from prying eyes.

We went to a nearby pub that was cramped and crowded enough to be private. Nevertheless, my lapse of control bothered me, and I just wanted to go home and massage my ego.

Unfortunately, no get out clause was available, as a couple vacating a table offered us their seats, so we sat down. I felt awkward.

I was concocting a realistic explanation for my tears when he came straight to the point and said, "Ellen, I know you've been involved with Derek Townsend."

That was a bolt from the blue. Embarrassed, I stood up to leave.

"It isn't common knowledge. Sit down…please. I need to talk to you as your manager."

I sat down as a tear ran down my nose. He noticed and produced another tissue. "At this rate I should invest in tissues," he said as he got up. "Do you want a drink?"

"A tonic water, please."

I watched him walk to the bar. It was busy, so it gave me time to think. I wondered how he knew about the affair. We'd been discreet, although I realised with hindsight, not for my benefit.

Mr Bennet was back quicker than I expected, and I wasn't looking forward to hearing what he had to say. He'd bought himself a whisky. I hoped he didn't feel he needed it.

He didn't waste words. "Your personal life is your business. However, my concern is that it may cause a problem within the team."

I was beginning to wish I had ordered whisky, too. "It's over, finished. There is no problem," I said.

He sighed before he dropped the bombshell. "Derek seems to think there may be, and you are still visibly upset. You have to find a way to work with him and be part of his team. If not..."

My face burning, I said, "If not? What's that supposed to mean?"

“Look, Ellen, you’re a valued member of staff. Having said that, the M D is very impressed with Derek’s presentation, and his innovative ideas have brought Terversal back on board. Whatever he wants, he gets. Do you understand what I’m saying?”

That did it. I blurted everything out like a waterfall in full flow. The guilt and shame of the affair, and the biggy: finding out Derek had just used me to steal my layout and ideas for the Terversal Industries advertising account.

Mr Bennett sat listening to me, his face impassive. After I finished talking I felt empty, useless and silly.

“Have you any proof?” he asked.

I laughed and shook my head. “I can’t use it.”

“Why not?”

“Why not? Do you know about my husband?”

“I know he’s sick.”

“He’s a good man. Derek said he’d tell him about us if I said anything. So there it is.”

“Will you tell your husband?”

“I don’t know. But I do know I can do my job, whatever it takes. I need this job. I’ll toe the line.”

He finished his whisky and stood up. “See you do, and consider telling your husband. Blackmail doesn’t go away, and it sleeps until needed.”

That was ten months ago. It’s been difficult but I’m feeling better, thanks to hearing the office whispers:

‘Terversal is pressing for the New year layout.’

‘He’s been given two weeks to come up with something.’

‘He sits in his office all day, staring at the walls.’

My spirits rose on seeing the Managing Director's face develop a droop. I wondered how he viewed his golden boy then.

It was nearly deadline day and I hoped Derek was feeling as desperate as he looked. He sauntered over to my desk. I had known he would eventually. The cretin smiled at me, and I made damn sure he saw me cover my work.

"Ellen, you busy?"

Oh, those dulcet tones! Did they really once make my heart race? I stifled a giggle, noticing him squinting at my paperwork.

"Aren't we all?" I quipped.

He had an avaricious gleam in his eyes. I followed his line of vision to where I'd not quite covered the entire layout I'd been working on. He would have seen the logo 'Terversal Industries'. I felt a tickle of excitement, like a hunter waiting for his prey, and if he'd leaned over any more he'd have fallen over.

"Working on a new layout, I scc?"

How could I ever have let those lips kiss me, and whisper endearments? I inwardly shuddered at the thought, and then gave the Oscar performance of the year, casually saying, "Just in case. You never know."

About half an hour later the fire alarm sounded, and everyone vacated the building, assembling in the car park. After roll call, I noticed Derek was missing. I guessed where he'd gone.

It was a good thirty minutes before they decided it had been a fault in the system, and we were allowed back in.

Derek was back in the office. I took one look at my desk. My layout had been rearranged. I glared at him just enough to make him flush, and I took comfort in the thought he may have strained something rushing upstairs.

But on the day of his presentation something more serious than a strain caught up with him.

The Terversal representatives departed in stony silence. The M D had a go at Derek, and the company secretary very obligingly left the intercom on. Every word rang throughout the office.

“You’ve made us look fools! Get out of my sight, and out of the agency.”

He came into the office to clear his desk, stopping at mine to deliver his final barb. “You set me up, you bitch.”

You could have heard a pin drop. Whoever said revenge was sweet was bloody right. I glanced over at Mr Bennet, the manager. He nodded and, with everyone hanging on to my words, I said, “Derek, you should have done your homework, then you would have known what you stole was the presentation that lost us the Terversal account five years ago.”

Afterwards I did wonder about the fire alarms. I didn’t have anything to do with that, but it was dammed convenient. I later found out Mr Bennet had worked for the Fire Brigade many years before.

But I won’t ask.

MERMAID OF THE MIND

Ann Cooper

Do you remember, when we were young,
Golden days and bright blue skies,
Holidays by the sea,
Wavelets licking at the beach,
Scuttling crabs, smooth shiny pebbles, painted shells?
Do you remember?
Today the world is bleak,
Angry storm clouds, lashing rain,
Clashing waves spitting out their frothing venom.
I shiver and watch,
Remembering the sunshine days.
Suddenly I see brown, fronded hair.
There, there—a glimpse of shining tail.
Logic tells me it is not so,
But I know, I know.
Once again the magic of my childhood
Dances in my soul.

THE MUTALITY MAN

HarryRiley

"Lift latch on t'door Kev-lad, its only Arthur Smithers, Co-op-mutality-man, come for his weekly half crown."

A thin, pasty-faced man entered, dressed in an ill-fitting, pinstriped suit, using a walking stick to support his damaged knee. He skidded slightly on a wet patch on the floor, his left leg clicking loudly on the uneven quarry tiles, as he awkwardly thrust it forward with each lurching movement.

The young boy who ran to obey his grandmother's command to let in the diminutive male visitor, stared open-mouthed at the man's noisy lower limb, and seemed incapable of speech.

From her comfortable seat by the warm glow of the black oven-range, where she sat peeling potatoes, old Enid Kelly reached out a blotched and flabby arm to greet the new arrival, and pointed to an upright chair by the pine table.

"Sit thisen down, Arthur, and tek yer weight off thet gammy leg o' yourn. Money's on't table, all ready for yuh. Jenny's payin'. She's struggling to mek ends meet, all on her own, since Frank cleared off wi' his fancy piece, blonde Lucetta Cornbright from three doors away. My gal's gonna be workin' extra hours at the bakery from now on, to get Kevin's new school uniform."

Thankfully, the collector did as he was bid and, sitting down, reached into his inside jacket pocket to bring out an official-looking slim, blue book, with a pencil attached to it by a short length of cord. For some reason known only to himself, he licked the lead point, before scribbling onto a columned page.

He then scooped up the large, round, silver coin and dropped it into the leather money-pouch suspended from his belt, to clink loudly amongst its other cousins.

"Would you like a cup o'tea, Arthur? I've just put kettle on, and Jenny'll be back any minute to mek it for yer."

Stretching out his damaged leg and re-pocketing the payment book, the Co-operative Mutual collector grinned and thanked the old lady, adding that this was his last call of the evening, and that he was grateful to be inside and out of the cold weather.

"Aye, Ma, a cuppa would do grand. I've got some new pills and could do wi' tekin' one wi' a drink, thanks. This leg's really giving me some grief."

Making a half turn of her head in her visitor's direction, dipping both hands into the water-filled bowl, and selecting another brown tuber, the woman changed the topic of conversation. "Have they caught the young varmint that crippled you?"

"No, Ma, and not likely to, either—no witnesses. He came at me from behind. I never knew what happened. Clobbered me with a heavy, leaded sock or some such, and I was down on floor in a jiffy, smashing me knee-cap, and he'd fled wi' me tally bag. All I noticed was his head was covered wi' a hood, and face wi' a scarf up to his eyes." The speaker fingered his replacement leather moneybag and explained it was now tied to his belt to keep it more secure.

The normally placid old lady was scathing with her condemnation. "They're too soft wi' 'em these days. If I had my way I'd lash 'em to a wheel and throw knives at 'em. They'd never do it agin, I know!"

Conversation stopped as Kevin's sturdy young mother arrived, deftly throwing her dark grey duffle coat up onto a vacant wooden peg behind the door.

The collector secretly reflected that he'd have run off in Frank's place too, if he'd had such a monstrous woman as Jenny to come home to. To his mind she was physically a younger version of her mother, with very few outwardly appealing features to commend her. He just hoped she had other virtues that she kept well hidden.

"Ah, there you are, Jenny. Mek us all a cup o' tea, will yuh? Arthur's got to go in a minute, and I'm busy gettin' dinner ready."

Grumbling moodily under her breath, as she picked up the tea-pot and reached for the whistling kettle, Jenny roughly thrust aside her son, Kevin, who'd been sitting on the rug, quietly tweaking his latest matchbox acquisition: a live, hard-shelled, black beetle with horns and multiple twitching legs.

Swiftly clearing an area of the table for tea-making space, Jenny acknowledged Arthur with a brief nod, and asked him if his wedding was still going ahead the following week, despite his accident.

Instinctively rubbing his injured limb, the tallyman vehemently replied: "But of course, Jen. I won't let me plans be disrupted. Angie's one in a million and I'm luckiest fellow around. I'm still able to walk, and I'll get her down St. Martin's aisle, somehow. I take it you're both still coming?"

Enid replied first: "Oh, yes, Arthur, if these old legs'll carry me. We like weddings, don't we, Jenny love?"

Staying longer than he'd intended, the collector was drawn into deeper conversation, especially by Jenny, about his forthcoming nuptials, and honeymoon in Blackpool, and it was already growing dark before he was out the door and making his way home.

Soon he approached Quarry Park, a notorious, downbeat warren of concrete bed-sits, where the local council had taken to re-housing many problem-families, and close to where his attacker had pounced. Filled with apprehension, he wished there was a little more daylight and more people about.

Turning a corner it happened again, and down went the rounds-man a second time. Even though he'd been half expecting it, and the heavy head-blow was deflected onto his shoulder as he twisted, he hit the pavement with a thud. Then greedy hands frantically searched for his cash-bag and a knife hacked away at his money belt, as he helplessly tried to defend himself.

Seconds later it was all over and, again, the culprit scuttled away, leaving the victim dazed on the floor, minus his dignity and his cash-bag. As on the previous occasion, no words had been spoken by the offender.

Later, discussing this attack from a hospital bed, where he was being treated for superficial knife wounds to his hands, and undergoing tests for concussion, Arthur agreed with the police sergeant that the perpetrator must have been watching his movements, ready to strikc at the most opportune moment.

"No, Officer, it all happened so fast," he replied in his normal voice, no longer feeling the need to put on an accent. "One minute I was striding along, minding my own business and the next, I was knocked to the floor, with this heavy knee pressing on my stomach, crushing the wind out of me, and a blade was hacking away at my belt. I thought I was being stabbed to death, and I tried to ward off the blows with my hands. That's why they got cut so much. I begged him not to kill me, but he never spoke."

Arthur hoisted himself more upright from his sitting position in the bed and pointed with his bandaged right hand to a plate on the medicine cabinet, where lay a small object. "All I managed to grab and hold onto was that wooden toggle from his coat..." A sudden thought struck him as he stared, stupefied, at the well-worn, oval, brown toggle with the hole in the middle, and from which hung a frayed piece of cord. "No, impossible, it can't be…?"

The policeman, sitting by the injured man's bedside, lifted his gaze from the notebook, where he'd been busily writing down a statement.

"You were saying, sir?"

Sadly the victim shook his head. "Find the coat with the missing toggle, Officer, and you'll have my attacker, and I know just the place to look."

A visit by the police to Enid Kelly's humble abode, with Arthur in tow, brought a look of shocked amazement from the old girl's daughter as they explained they had a warrant to search the premises. Jenny's expression quickly turned to disgust as the older female officer asked Enid to vacate her fireside chair, so she might look under her cushion. The old woman painfully lifted her stiff body upright and, with the aid of her daughter, managed to hobble to the empty chair by the table.

She gave Arthur Smithers a meaningful look and asked him what he meant by bringing the law to her door. "Go on Arthur, tell 'em it wasn't us that attacked you. Why, you're practically one o' the family. We couldn't do a thing like that. We're going to your wedding, for Heaven's sake!"

Still groggy, the collector supported himself in the entrance doorway as he answered, "Well, wedding's been postponed indefinitely, or at least until I'm declared fit and well again. I bin put on sick-list for three weeks."

An inspection of the armchair revealed no hidden clues, and Enid was allowed to resume her seat. Ann Ward, the other WPC, had drifted off to the parlour and her excited voice came loudly, calling urgently for her comrade to join her there.

Arthur waited with baited breath until both women officers came back, the senior policewoman carrying a dark bundle of outer clothing. It appeared to be a hooded duffle coat, the type of hardwearing garment universally popular for both sexes in those mid 1960s. She triumphantly delved into a deep patch pocket on the front and withdrew a heavy, sand-filled woollen sock, dripping wet sand onto the rug. The coat seemed to have a missing toggle, and the WPC compared the one she'd brought along with the existing ones. She had a perfect match.

Fumbling around the outer edges of the other front pocket, the confident expression on the searcher's face confirmed to the watchers that she had located something else of immense interest, which she had no intentions of extracting. "What's this, then? Feels like a knife. We'll know better when forensics have examined it for fingerprints."

She carefully handed the clothing back to WPC Ward and, turning to face Jenny Kelly, she read out an official caution, and asked her to accompany them to the blue and white Panda car parked outside. They departed, leaving old Enid, head bent forward, sobbing into her handkerchief, and with the young boy, Kevin, fearfully clinging to her apron strings.

Arthur Smithers sat in the rear of the Little Ford Anglia beside Jenny Kelly on the short journey to the local police station. She protested her innocence until the senior WPC asked her not to comment until the official interview would be convened.

In the presence of Detective Sergeant Colin Melville and WPC Ann Ward, the first of a series of interviews with Jennifer Kelly was conducted.

Yes, the young mother admitted the dark grey duffle belonged to her and that the steak knife with the wooden handle and the serrated-blade had been part of a set of knives belonging to her household.

Under the most severe and unrelenting questioning by the detective, she stuck to her story, that from the moment Arthur Smithers had departed on that fateful day, she had stayed with her young son and his gran, and that Enid would surely be able to back up her story.

However, the fingerprints extracted from the steak knife handle compared perfectly with those taken at the station from the coat's owner, and she was still their number one suspect.

Jennifer Kelly was later remanded into police custody whilst her alibi could be checked out.

"Of course, sir, the old girl is going to back up her daughter. What else would you expect? She claims Jenny never left the house that evening, not even for a moment, just as her daughter insisted to us at the interview. We have motive: she was in dire straights financially, since her common-law hubby abandoned her for his flighty piece down the road. We have means: the steak knife contained a perfect set of her own fingerprints, and the blade was covered in a blood-match for Smithers.

To cap it all we have opportunity: the attack happened only streets away from her home, from where their visitor had just left. Also, she knew he'd be carrying a fair amount of cash, having concluded his round." Detective Sergeant Melville's face was puce with anger as he discussed the Smithers case with Police Inspector Andy Walker at the station.

Inspector Walker left his desk and turned his back on his fellow officer, staring out of the office window at the maze of urban rooftops, as if for inspiration.

"I am still not convinced, Colin, it's all too easy. With all this damning evidence you still could not break her story, and yet... I think both women are keeping something from us. Go back to Enid Kelley and take that young constable, Ann Ward, with you. She's bright, and might just pick up on something we've missed."

The sergeant acquiesced and was given an additional warning: "Be careful though, none of your heavy bull-in-a-china-shop tactics. We don't want to be seen to be bullying a frail old woman. The press would have a field day."

The Inspector stopped Melville in the doorway just as he was leaving. "By the way, I've just heard some shocking news. Our victim, Arthur Smithers, will not be returning to work, after all. He was rushed to hospital last night with a suspected stroke, as a result of his injuries no doubt, and died in the early hours. This has now become a murder case."

Enid Kelly was beside herself with grief on hearing the news that the co-op collector had passed away, and that her daughter could be facing a murder charge. Sergeant Melville waited impatiently for the old woman to calm down, and then attempted to unravel her previous statement, but she stuck to her guns.

Her tears upset her grandson so much that he screamed out: "You leave my Gran alone!" and bravely waded into battle, walloping the sergeant repeatedly on the leg with his toy tractor. The policeman gave up, apologised, and wisely escorted his young colleague out of the house.

As they later sat in the police car, Sergeant Melville had to admit to WPC Ward that he was stumped.

"I'd like to come down really hard on them both, with a bit of third degree, but my hands are tied and, in any case, I'm sure we have enough for a prosecution, without digging any further…in spite of what Andy Walker says."

His young companion shook her head. "I'm thinking Sarge…what was it Enid said to Kevin when he began bashing you on the leg with his toy? She didn't call him by his real name. I'm sure she said stop-it, Gus!"

Slumped dejectedly in the driving seat, the detective swung his head round to stare at his uniformed colleague, and then thumped the steering wheel in delight. "By heck, Ward, you're right. How could I have missed that? You're a bloody marvel-woman!"

Undeterred by this unexpected praise, WPC Ward continued with her train of thought. "Now if there is a male called Gus, where can we find out, without alerting the suspects?"

Sergeant Melville started his Cortina engine and swung the car into a u-turn. "Let's try Etwell's Grocers on the corner. They get all the local gossip, and are sure to know."

His hunch proved right. Barry Etwell knew all about Gus Kelly. "Aye, Gus is a regular, he often pops in early doors for his fags and matches. He works nights and sleeps during the day. Bit of a fly customer, though. I have to watch him like a hawk, or he'd be away with half my shop. According to Enid, he's never got enough money, spends it all on drink and cards. Check your own records. I'm sure you'll have him on file somewhere."

Back at the police station things began to fall into place, and a petty thief with the name of Gus Kelly soon came to light. As a young tearaway he'd run with the Fletchers, a gang of hotheads, who had only been broken up when Detective Police Sergeant Andy Walker (as he had been then) had put Errol Fletcher away. He'd received seven years for GBH.

With a record of minor pilfering behind him, Gus Kelly appeared to have settled down as he had grown older, and nothing more had been heard of him since.

However, with a string of unsolved personal assaults in the district, going back over two years, it seemed likely the police might have a possible candidate to pursue for those offences as well.

A hasty conference was called and, as a confirmed member of the team, WPC Ann Ward was invited by Andy Walker to sit in on the meeting.

They would swoop on Gus Kelly the very next morning, just as he finished his shift as a lathe operator at the giant bicycle factory. That way it would cause no extra upheaval for his mother, Enid.

However, as the workers flooded out of the tall, double gates, Gus Kelly was nowhere to bc seen.

His foreman complained he had not clocked in, and they'd had to bring in someone else to cover for his shift at great inconvenience. A check back at his home confirmed their new chief suspect had flown the coop.

Jennifer Kelly was released from police custody and warned she could later face a charge of obstructing police enquiries, if the prosecution service decided to take action against her.

Three months later, during the search of a vacant warehouse, after an anonymous tip off, WPC Ann Ward was temporarily separated from her senior colleagues as she quietly searched the basement. A slight scuffling sound directed her torch beam onto a pile of sacking in a corner.

As she unwittingly bent down to pull away the top covering, a large unwashed and unshaven male leaped up, causing her to scream out. A large hand grabbed her by the throat, and a pair of wild eyes stared back at her, as the assailant's other hand emerged, brandishing a fully-extended clasp knife. Then she was spun around as her attacker took control and pulled her even closer so she had her back to him.

Instinctively WPC Ward knew this man was the missing Gus Kelly. The distinct smell of heavy engineering oil from the man's dirty overalls and close proximity filled her nostrils, turning her stomach.

Her startled cry had alerted her two male comrades, Officers Melville and Walker, and both came bounding down the stairs from the upper floors which they had been searching. Andy Walker immediately weighed up the situation and cursed his folly in putting the young female officer in harm's way.

He remembered Gus Kelly from years before, as a little streetwise toe-rag, but who had now grown into a hefty fifteen stone muscular adult. The inspector called out in an authoritative tone: "Now don't be silly, lad, put your weapon down and let the officer go. You're in enough trouble already, don't make it any worse."

Kelly had both huge fists around WPC Ward's slender neck and he yelled out a vicious warning: "Back off, or I'll do her in. I mean it!" To add emphasis to his threat, he nicked his captive's throat with the point of his blade, before letting his knife-hand return to his side.

The watchers got the message, as a trickle of bright red blood oozed down his victim's throat and over his other hand, still clutched around her neck.

Pretty, dark-haired WPC Ann Ward was known by her male colleagues in the force as the 'Belle of Corton Street

Nick'. There was not one amongst them who would have hesitated to lay down his life for her. She would not have weighed more than nine stone wet through, but as her two male companions reluctantly obeyed the criminal's commands and stepped away, what happened next was simply unbelievable, and was to have far reaching effects on police training and defensive tactics for over a decade, earning WPC Ward a commendation for bravery.

Observing the three Judo principles of *Movement, Balance and Leverage* to overcome a much stronger opponent, Ann Ward sprang into action.

Gus Kelly never had a clue. Using both hands, she grasped the arm around her throat, to try and loosen his grip, and then ducking low and forward, using her back as a fulcrum, she pivoted him over her own body, turning his much greater strength and weight against him. He landed flat out on the hard concrete floor, the wind and fight knocked out of him.

Her two colleagues stared at one another, amazed, and then at this thin stripling of a girl, who'd just tossed a fully-grown man over her shoulders, as though it was something she did every day, and could do so a thousand times more.

Andy Walker hardly recognised his own voice as it came out in a hoarse cough: "By crikey, Melville, was that for real, or am I dreaming?"

Gus Kelly pleaded guilty to both attacks on Arthur Smithers, the Co-operative rounds-man, and exonerated his mother Enid and sister Jenny of any blame or complicity in his unlawful activities. He admitted he had been responsible for six other attacks, and named the victims.

He said he'd been upstairs, asleep in his bedroom, when he'd been awakened by voices downstairs and recognised that the tallyman, Smithers, had called for his money.

Knowing the visitor would have a full moneybag, having finished his round, Gus Kelly had slipped downstairs immediately after Smithers had left. Surreptitiously collecting a steak knife from the cutlery drawer he'd then grabbed his sister's duffle coat, just as he'd done many times before, telling the women he was nipping out to get some more cigarettes. Once outside, he'd quickly filled an old sock with wet sand from Kevin's garden sandpit and had tied a knot in the top. This had made a suitable club. Quietly stalking the limping Arthur Smithers for a few streets, using the fast enveloping darkness for cover, he had then walloped him from behind and cut away the cash-bag, thinking no one would be any the wiser.

Pleading mitigation, his defence lawyer blamed his client's earlier allegiance with the Fletchers' gang for his bad start in life and this, together with having no father to guide him along the straight and narrow, had led to his downfall. Ernest Kelly had deserted Enid, leaving the boy and his sister to grow up as best they could.

This cut no ice with the courts and Gus Kelly was put away for manslaughter.

Over a celebratory drink at the Golden Ball, their local watering hole, WPC Ann Ward was quizzed by her two male colleagues, Walker and Melville, as to how she'd acquired the skills to tackle a much heavier opponent.

Embarrassed by being questioned about something she'd been taught to do instinctively, Ann sought to explain, without going into lengthy details. Seeking advice from her gym instructor, she'd wisely enrolled in a club for martial arts. With blood running down her front and a brutal thug's hot breath threatening to engulf her, she'd put months of hard, grinding practice into action, just as she had been taught. And luckily it had worked.

A WALK ON THE WILD SIDE

Mike Hemstock

Whilst walking in a field one day
Towards the "Shipley Boat,"
I came across an unusual sight,
A sweet, white nanny goat.

Now, I'm not a naturalist at heart,
And, although it may sound silly,
It wasn't until it charged at me,
I realised it was a billy.

Entering into another field,
Rubbing my aching buttocks,
Ahead, I saw a herd of cows,
But soon saw they were bullocks.

After I'd run as fast as I could,
And my nerves were once more settled,
I walked into a farmyard,
Straight through a bunch of nettles.

I found some dock leaves straightaway,
And was looking for somewhere to sit,
To rub my stinging legs with them,
But then I had a fit.

I'd sat on a hill to soothe my legs,
A hill that was full of ants;
Me, wearing only a pair of shorts,
They were crawling inside my pants.

Running towards the canal bank,
I jumped in with a splash.
It was then that I remembered,
Canal water gives me a rash.

I dragged myself out of the drink,
And sat on the bank to dry,
Overcome with weariness,
I thought I'd have some shuteye.

So, then I lay me down to rest,
Under the clear blue sky,
But waking a short while later,
I was startled by a fly.

Though it wasn't a fly that had startled me,
But a great big bumble bee,
Flying about and buzzing around,
And it landed on my knee.

I wondered whether to leave it,
In the hope it would go away,
But as you probably know by now,
This was not my lucky day.

I swatted it and wafted it,
But still it buzzed around.
Waving my arms in desperation,
I knocked it to the ground.

As it lay reeling on the floor,
I did a foolish thing.
I went and put my foot on it,
To incapacitate its sting.

You see, this was a Queen Bee,
And its mates were very angry.
Very soon, I was surrounded,
And they started to harangue me.

There was no option but run away,
To the safest place around,
So, to rid myself of this swarm of bees,
Into the water again did I bound.

But I soon jumped out of there once more,
From the foul smell that was so bad,
Because the canal had not been dredged,
Ever since I'd been a young lad.

I had sticklebacks wriggling in my pants,
The ones with the spiky fin.
I had to take my shorts off,
Exposing my sunburned skin.

To top it all there came a barge,
Out on a Sunday cruise,
And there was I, showing all my glory,
In nothing but my birthday suit.

The passengers stood and laughed at me,
Making me feel so shy.
Why did this have to happen to me?
Pray tell me, why, oh, why?

Quick as a flash I grabbed my shorts,
Hurtling away to the rushes.
There I found to my dismay,
I'd landed in a patch of rose bushes.

I was so scratched and oh, so sore,
I didn't know what to do.
I decided to make my weary way back,
By taking a short cut or two.

As I approached the turning,
To take the shortest route home,
I stumbled onto the tarmac,
Grazing my elbow to the bone.

My day was totally ruined,
As far as I was concerned.
The only thing that I wanted then,
Was home with a safe return.

As I hurried on, as fast as I could,
Crossing roads without a fuss,
Thinking what else could happen to me,
I was knocked down by a bus.

I was taken by an ambulance,
For surgery with a knife.
I used to be a **HUSBAND,**
But now…I am a **WIFE.**

If someone says to me one day,
"Take a walk on the wild side",
I'd quite politely say to them,
"No thanks, I'll stay inside".

THE CRACKED POT

David Brailsford

This delightful story has its origins in China.

An elderly Chinese couple owned a small paddy field, growing enough rice to provide them with a meagre living. They would collect water for cooking from the river in two large pots, which hung either end of a pole, carried across the shoulders.

One of them was perfect, always delivering a full portion of water, but the other had a crack in it.

At the end of the long walk from the stream to the house, the cracked pot lost much of its load, arriving home half-full.

For many years, this went on daily, with the woman only bringing home one and a half pots of water.

They could not afford to buy a new one.

The perfect pot was always boasting about its usefulness.

The cracked one said to the woman, "I'm ashamed of my imperfection, miserable that I lose half of my contents on the way home.

The old woman smiled and replied, "Do you not notice there are flowers growing on your side of the path and none growing on the other pot's side? That's because I've always known how you leak, so I have planted seeds on your side of the path...not on the intact pot's side."

Every day, as she walked home, the flawed pot watered them.

Laughing, the old woman gleefully said, "For the last two years, I've been able to pick lovely flowers to grace our humble table. Without your flaw this wouldn't have been possible. My husband and I thank you so much for the beauty you bring to our home."

Everyone has their own unique flaws and cracks. It is often these that make our lives together so interesting and rewarding.

Take each person for what they are and look for the good in them.

So, to all my crackpot friends, have many happy days, remembering to smell the flowers on your side of the path.

Show this to any crackpot friend you have and see if they smile.

Lastly, don't forget this CRACKPOT who gave you this little gem.

CLANDESTINE MEETINGS

Barrrie J Kinsella

It all began one day at the library when I was researching for a tricky A level in philosophy. My school, it seemed, had scant material for what I wanted so, armed with a list of relevant authors, there I was, Joey Martin, sitting quietly at a desk in the reading room.

At sixteen and three quarters I was as observant as any teenager with rampant hormones, so I couldn't help noticing a girl nearby, partly obscured by an impressive pile of books on the desk in front of her. Light-haired but not blonde, in my expert opinion a year or two younger than me, she sat making notes in a writing pad.

Reluctantly, I returned my attention to my work, to be interrupted by a series of loud bangs, caused by the books toppling off the girl's desk.

Like a shot, I was out of my seat, gathering up the nearest volumes. Unfortunately, she had the same idea, and we met in a collision which deposited us both on the floor.

Apologising, I helped her up, along with the rest of her books. Naturally, she was flustered, but effusive in her thanks. Close to, she was definitely attractive, cornflower-blue eyes, with a slight flush covering her fair complexion.

With everything restored onto her desk, we were left looking at one another.

"My name's Joey," I said.

"And mine's Sheila," she replied.

Conversation evolved naturally. Sheila was studying English Literature, so we had a lot in common.

From that day on we met at the library at least twice a week, comparing notes in whispers, despite the loud shushing from the spinster library assistant.

Sheila attended the girls' high school on the edge of town. It crossed my mind to wonder why it didn't have the books she required, for it had the reputation of being 'upper class', far above the one I attended.

Our first date was to an open-air jazz concert on the local park; most enjoyable, but Sheila insisted on catching the bus home by herself, which I thought strange.

I was intrigued by Sheila Jones.

Then, one day, all was revealed, almost by accident. The local paper ran a front page article and photograph of Peter Jones, the well-known industrialist, and chairman of the governors at the high school, opening their new science laboratory which he had funded as a gift. I read and reread the article. I couldn't believe my eyes. He was Sheila's dad!

The semi-secrecy of our meetings was explained. I realised I'd never met any of her friends. Our meetings had been virtually clandestine on her part.

Sheila knew something was wrong when we met again. "But, Joey," she sobbed, "Father would never have approved of me going out with you."

"Especially with me coming from the wrong side of the tracks," I snarled.

She looked at me. "Joey, I loved you from the first moment I saw you in the library. I'd seen you weeks before, and wondered how to speak to you."

I broke in, "And then you had the idea of pushing that pile of books over, knowing I would come to the rescue?"

She nodded tearfully.

Silently, I rose to my feet and walked out of the library.

Years later, I heard that Sheila had married the son from a titled family. I'm sure her father would have approved.

Me? I passed that A level. Very resilient, the Martin family.

I still think about Sheila, together with the words 'clandestine meetings' and now understand the meaning, although, as you know, I was totally innocent of them at the time.

FIRST IMPRESSIONS

Shirley McIntyre

As usual, I was drooling over the pudding menu. Having wolfed down a Caesar Salad, lightly drizzled in low-fat mayonnaise, I was still Hank Marvin. My sweet tooth demanded 'naughty but nice'.

It was one of those early spring days when some hardy souls ignored the perishing winds and their goose-pimply flesh. The sun had got its hat on and that called for flimsy summer clothes, whilst others—thin-blooded, nesh-nellies—still snuggled in winter coats. I thought I'd settled somewhere in between with my navy Damart fleece. A satisfactory compromise.

Which pudding to choose, however, was a different kettle of fish (or kettle of desserts). Whatever, my sweet tooth was not up for compromising. No settling for mediocrity or second best, hence the cogitating and, I'm loath to admit, unattractive drooling.

My first thought, in view of my decision to dress warmly, was to plump for a school-dinner type of pudding (if you'll excuse this paradox). Treacle sponge and custard was tempting, but then so was spotted dick, and bread and butter pudding. I swear I could feel those warm custardy sultanas rolling around my tongue. My stomach rumbled, and my sweet tooth became noticeably needy.

Glancing around, I spotted a muscular fellow on the next table. It wasn't his designer cut-off vest and Paul Smith shorts, revealing various intricate tattoos, that caught my attention. What struck me was what can only be described as the ecstatic expression on his face as he slurped his chosen pud.

It looked wonderful. A tall proud sundae glass, brimming with juicy strawberries, ice cream and other anonymous delights. I scoured the menu for a picture of this heavenly dessert, and found it: 'Eton Mess'. It was in that column of 'Summer Specials' that I'd dismissed, due to my pessimism over the weather. I looked at the picture, and then to Mr Flimsy's nearly empty sundae glass. He still had that euphoric look. It was a no-brainer. Eton Mess it had to be.

Relieved at having made the decision, I went to the counter. "An Eton Mess, please."

"Banana, strawberry, or peach?" smiled the assistant.

"Oh, strawberry, please." I salivated at the thought of those strawberries, ice cream, and the mystery of the anonymous ingredient.

"£1.50, please."

Eton Mess arrived. My first taste—yummy. I shared and embraced Mr Flimsy's ecstasy. Eton Mess was to die for. Strawberries, cream, ice cream and—that sneaky hidden bonus—meringue. If Flimsy's face was ecstatic, then mine was orgasmic. I slurped my way down, relishing each mouthful.

Finally, tragically, I reached the end. The grand finale. A luscious-looking, lonesome ice-coated strawberry, encased in a sliver of meringue beckoned. Bliss. But then, oh, my God, what was that? What was that ear-splitting bang? Was a sniper on the loose? Had the ceiling fallen in?

Panic stricken, I looked around at my fellow diners, seemingly oblivious to this catastrophic disaster. Then I realised I was the only one who could hear the deafening crack. My top front tooth had given up the ghost and snapped, unceremoniously defeated by a frozen strawberry.

The next morning I made an appointment with Mr Molar in the High Street—Dazzling Dentures a Speciality—for my first impression...

AN OTTER'S LAMENT

Angela Rigley

The sun glistens brightly on the undisturbed lake;
I dive through its shimmering surface.
But what will I find for my family to eat
In the dank, murky weeds of this place?

'Twas once a safe haven, and teeming with life,
Happy voices and songs they would ring.
But now it's a danger, a site most avoid,
Where no baby cubs play, or birds sing.

They say it's polluted, befouled and defiled,
An odious mixture of muck.
Full of chemicals that have poisoned most things,
From the fish, to the heron and duck.

I'd better get out, there's nothing in here
For me to take back to my holt.
My babes might be dead, my wife may be too,
And I 'spose it is all my own fault.

It's been much too long since they had a good meal,
No carp, trout or eels remain now.
But where can I go? My homeland is here.
Find strange lands? I wouldn't know how.

I've tried very hard to find food for them all.
I should have moved out weeks ago,
But my own selfish pride told me, 'Stay where you are'.
Now all I have left is my woe.

But what's that I hear? My wife with my pups.
She's calling out, running towards me.
She's found a fresh stream. Oh, my troubles are o'er.
We can live now, in safe harmony.

JACK-IN-THE-B0X

Dawn raffle

The sandwich board standing on the pavement attracted me; the name written on it conjured up the promise of surprise: JACK-IN-THE-BOX.

Underneath, a large arrow pointed into an alleyway. I was hooked. I had to take a peek.

A neat courtyard belied the busy street behind me. Small, yet amazingly spacious, it had a Dickensian air. The cobblestones, enhancing the various ceramics, were filled with plants, flowers and crockery items around the open door. Enticed and intrigued, I had to go in.

I entered to find I was no longer in Ripley, a small town in Derbyshire. I had stepped into yesteryear.

To describe it as an emporium would be right, as a curiosity shop definitely. Either would do. Inside the doorway a selection of hats caught my eye. Some looked nineteen-twenty style, reminding me of flapper girls, and I wondered where they had been worn, and what tales they had to tell.

In contrast, flat irons, large and small, reminded me of my grandmother's warm kitchen with the old fashioned cast-iron cooking range. A doll's house, waiting to be owned again, stood nearby, amongst tables and shelves laden with memorabilia from every walk of life.

An assistant smiled in acknowledgement. However, I was left to browse, pick up and examine bits and pieces. I leafed through a pile of comics, then some knitting patterns. I smiled at the old money price: 3/6d. A wave of nostalgia surfaced, memories of childhood savoured, giving a sense of a time without haste.

It isn't a big place, nonetheless, space is well used without being cluttered, and I was pleasantly surprised when an aroma of coffee drifted through.

Following the source, I discovered the teashop, displaying cakes and deserts to make the mouth water. Several customers were enjoying meals and the atmosphere was relaxed and friendly. It was picture-perfect, and is well worth a visit.

I have told my family and friends about Jack-in-the-box. Maybe it won't be everyone's cup of tea. But it was mine.

This poem was written soon after the murder of Sarah Payne, the murder that led to 'Sarah's Law'.

DEATH

Gordon F Butler

Is this the end,
Lying cold and dank in a field?
Why?
Why this one?
This field, this person?
What had happened
To bring this end?
Carefree, happily playing,
Then….
Then what?
You know,
Who did it knows,
But….
Do they know why?
In death
There should be dignity,
But to be left
Naked, despoiled,
To the ravages of nature.
This ignominy
Should not be.
Your family,
Hope gone,
But able now to say goodbye,
Though little solace
May help to curb the loss,
So out of time
And out of reason.

Who?
We might one day know.
Why?
Many reasons may be given,
But not one that could justify
The taking
Of one so innocent and young.

TIME MANAGEMENT

Annette Jones

I'm trying to get organised;
It's not an easy job;
I'm not a tidy person,
In fact I'm quite a slob!

I bought a book to help me
Just the other day;
It's full of good advice and tips
To get me underway.

I read about time management,
Prioritise each task,
At any given moment
This question I should ask:

What's the best thing I could do,
Right now, to be efficient?
And at the time of reading that
My sleep had been deficient.

So I decided there and then,
The best use of my time
Was have a kip, and so I did;
It really was sublime!

Time management's a doddle,
It really is a breeze!
I hope this book will help me
Tackle tidiness with such ease.

Sadly though, I doubt it,
I've struggled all my life
Against the messy piles of stuff,
A cause of marital strife.

I know my husband longs to see
The floor in every room,
But just the thought of clearing up
Fills my heart with gloom.

I really cannot face it,
It makes me feel so tired;
The book explains the reason why:
It's how my brain is wired.

It says I need a different way
To organise my stuff;
It must be easy, quick and fun,
Or I've just had enough.

It really understands me,
And so it must be true.
I hope that means that it will work;
My husband hopes so too.

I hate what they call "purging";
I just can't throw away;
I loath the thought of landfill,
It's pollution any day.

It's tricky, sorting paper,
Because I tend to write
Important notes or poems
On anything in sight.

I even used the inside
Of a toilet roll to scrawl
The first draft of a poem
That now I can't recall.

My husband must have chucked it,
And so it's lost forever;
My silly habit was to blame;
It really isn't clever.

I ought to write them down in books,
All kept in various places,
And yet the backs of envelopes
Are such attractive spaces.

It seems wasteful not to use them
When they're blank and just to hand,
And reusing beats recycling,
And does no harm to our land.

But I do want to get organised,
So I'll give it one more try,
And attack the clothing mountain
That makes my husband sigh.

The trouble with my wardrobe
Is all concerned with food,
For when you're putting weight on
It quite upsets your mood.

You have to buy new fat clothes,
As you just cannot squeeze in
To the ones you used to love to wear
When you were once so thin.

But you have to keep your thin clothes
As a goal of aspiration,
Yet now I've lost the weight again
I feel such elation.

I really want to celebrate,
And buy myself some more.
So, first I'll bag the old ones
To give to the charity store.

I'll get to that tomorrow,
I've done enough today.
I feel some more time management
Heading my weary way!

HIT THE FLOOR

David Brailsford.

Young Jenny and Robert Slater were on honeymoon, their first trip away from their home in England. They hired a car to visit famous and interesting places.

"I want to see New York," said Jenny, one morning. "Let's go there."

"Mmm...I don't know, love," her husband answered. "People say it's a dangerous place, and there may be strange characters wandering around."

"We shouldn't have any problems if we're careful," crooned Jenny.

So, early one evening, they arrived in the Big Apple and found a nice hotel.

Later, when they had settled in, they wandered into the streets and, not encountering any problems, Jenny said, "See, nothing to be afraid of."

They had dinner in a delightful restaurant, and then went to the cinema, arriving back at their hotel at midnight. The hotel had an underground garage, so they drove down and parked up. It was dark and spooky. "Where's the lift, Bob?"

"Over there, I think, near that door," he replied. "Come on, hurry up. I don't like this place."

A dark figure, leading a fierce-looking dog, emerged from behind a parked car. Nervously walking past him, the honeymoon couple rushed, post haste, to the lift door. They called the elevator and, after what seemed an eternity, the doors slid open. Jenny and Robert stumbled in and pressed the button to lift them to safety, but before the doors could close, the stranger and his growling dog jumped in.

Three people and a big black dog, together in a moving lift!

Thrusting his right hand deep into his jacket pocket, the ominous stranger whispered, “On the floor, girl.”

Trembling with fear, the couple dropped to the floor.

As the lift stopped, they rose and, handing their cash to the tall man, quickly ran to their room, locked the door behind them and reported the incident to the hotel receptionist. Police arrived and it was the early hours before they were able to get some fitful sleep.

After breakfast, they took the room key to the reception desk, where the girl said, “Sorry you had such a frightening experience in our beautiful city.”

“I think it's appalling to be robbed on our honeymoon,” complained Robert. “We won't ever be coming to New York again.”

Bowing to his anger, she gently replied, “I'm so sorry to hear that, but you won't be getting a bill. A tall gentleman with a nice dog paid for your room. Oh! Wait a minute, he left you this envelope.”

Robert carefully opened it and took out a letter. He read it out. *Here's your money and I'm so sorry my dog, Girl, frightened you in the lift last night.*

THE BLACK ANGEL

Ann Cooper

God felt the need to chill,
listening to His angels singing,
but all He could hear
were the bells of Heaven ringing.
"St. Peter, tell me the cause
of this tintinnabulation."
Eyes twinkling merrily,
He awaited revelation.
"Sir, it's the second highwayman,
the one called Johnny Cash.
All the bells are ringing
to celebrate his birthday bash."
God thought a while. "Ah! Of course!
Now I've got the crack.
He's my special angel
who insists on wearing black.
A humble man with love
and music in his soul,
livening up the angel choir
with a touch of rock and roll.
The gospel sure is hotter
and the country beat is strong,
and all the other angels
can't help but sing-a-long."
"You're right, sir and,
if you'll pardon the expression,
that Johnny Cash sure knows how
to knock 'em dead in Heaven!"

LILLY AND ELISA HELP FELICITY FOX
A Children's Story
Dianne Rasmussen

"What's that?" Lilly asked as she watched the brown creature crawl through the hedge.

"I don't know," her sister, Elisa, said. "But it looks tired and wet."

"Are you all right?" Lilly asked as she moved towards the animal, who was staring at her with wide-open eyes.

"You won't hurt me, will you? I'm Felicity Fox, and I've been chased by some men on horses and some barking dogs."

"We won't hurt you," the two girls said together.

"I'll look for a towel to dry you, and my sister will find you something to eat. Come on, Elisa." The two girls headed towards the house at the end of the garden.

Exhausted, Felicity Fox lay down on the grass and closed her eyes. She needed the rest after all that running to escape from the dogs. A little while later, she dragged herself to her feet as the two girls came back with a towel, and Lily dried off some of the water.

"How did you become so wet?"

"I had to swim along the river so the dogs couldn't smell where I'd gone," Felicity replied.

"That sounds horrible," Elisa said as she handed Felicity some pieces of chicken that her aunt had given her.

"Yes, how will you find your way home?" Lilly added.

Felicity Fox ate some of the chicken before answering, "I don't know, and I'm afraid the dogs will come again."

"Don't worry. I'll see if Auntie can think of anything," Lilly said as she turned to go indoors.

Elisa stayed with Felicity and they chatted as if they were life-long friends.

Lilly came back with her auntie, who went down on her knees and said, “Don’t worry, Felicity. We’ll try and help you find your way back to your home.”

“But what about the dogs?” Lilly asked.

“Ask some of your friends to help, and we’ll lay false trails.” Their aunt showed them a bag full of little grains of cat litter that she rubbed on the fox’s fur. “These smell of fox now and, if we lay a trail going in the wrong direction, the dogs will follow the false trail and we can take Felicity home safely.”

The two girls asked several friends to help, and several false trails were laid.

“That’s fooled the dogs,” laughed Elisa as they heard them in the distance, going in the opposite direction to the one Felicity had pointed out to them.

“Yes. Come on, let’s get Felicity Fox home,” said Lilly as she carried the red fox through the garden gate.

It was a long walk but then Felicity shouted, “That’s it. That’s my home,” as they came to a bush with the soil around it all roughed up.

Then a much bigger fox walked towards them and started making a loud howling noise. “It’s all right, Mum,” said Felicity. “These kind girls have brought me home.”

Lilly put Felicity down and she ran to her mother. “I nearly got caught by some horrid dogs, but these girls helped me, and they are my friends now. It was very frightening, but I’m glad I met them.”

Mummy Fox looked at Felicity to make sure she was all right and then turned to Lilly and Elisa. “Thank you. I hope we’ll see you again.”

"And, they must come and visit me." Felicity turned to Lilly and said, "You will come, won't you? And you too, Elisa?"

"Oh, yes," they both shouted. They all had a little hug and then Felicity and her mother joined the rest of their foxy family, who welcomed her home with shouts of glee.

Lilly and Elisa skipped home, happy they had helped their new friend.

MURDER ON MY MIND

Chrissie Lloyd

I shudder. Pre-meditated murder? Me? What would people think when and if they found out? Would they be surprised, saying, "Who would have thought such a shy, quiet girl was capable of such a thing?"

But can I really do it?

I don't want lots of blood. I'd vomit, and then faint. Blood's so messy, and I'd have to dispose of the weapon.

It might be murder, but I'd want it to be dignified.

I can't wait to have money in my bank account. It's been too long. Then there's the house, it must be worth a few hundred thousand.

I knock, and walk in. She's expecting me, and smiles. I feel guilty. "I've been thinking about you all night," I say truthfully. "Do you remember when I was little? You and Dad spoilt me. I was a mardy child; completely your fault."

Her arm reaches out and beckons me. "Come here beside me. Let's talk. Yes, you were a pretty child. I'd brush your hair till it shone, those long blonde ringlets. I was so upset when you cut your hair short."

I recall the pain and need to remind her. "There were always tangles, which hurt." I don't want to talk, not about when I was little, so why have I asked the question? I change the subject. "Where's Moggy? Have you fed her?"

"Moggy's fine. I need to say something to you. I know I've neglected you in the past, Kerry. I wish I could alter things, but we both know that's impossible."

"What's gone is gone." I feel impatient.

Please don't do this, not now.

"As you've got older, I've thought about the old days an awful lot."

"I'll make a drink." Why is she bringing up the old days, when I've finally syked myself up for murder?

"Thanks, love. Don't forget, two sugars for me."

Every time she reminds me. "Okay."

Holding her tea cup in both hands, she speaks. "You made me so proud, from when you brought home school drawings of trees that resembled spiders, right up to taking your A levels."

"That was a long while ago."

"You were six when you won the egg and spoon race."

"A very long while ago."

"I so wanted you to be a teacher, like me."

"Mother, I definitely wouldn't have had the patience for that."

"I cried when you got in with the wrong crowd."

"Okay, okay, don't remind me."

"We hardly talk. This conversation is overdue. You're my daughter. I love you. For better or for worse you'll always be my little girl."

"You'll have me in tears. I hate sentimentalism."

I'd thought we'd finished the talking last night. Hadn't she begged me; asked me to be the dutiful daughter?

"Have you changed your mind?" I ask. "I need to know."

"No, nothing will change my mind." Her hand grips mine. "I told you the pain is becoming unbearable. Some days are better than others, but only marginally."

"If you want to delay it, that's okay by me."

"No, definitely not. I just needed to tell you I love you."

Neither of us speaks. Just silence. But it's as if a drum is playing inside my head.

She inhales deeply. “I’m ready. Please do it quickly. I cannot stand the pain any more.”

I look at her, tears trickling down my cheeks. “I can’t do it, and you shouldn’t ask me. I’ll take you to Switzerland or some place that have professionals to do it. I don’t want the responsibility.”

How could I have imagined I could do such a thing?

PRIVATE, PRIVATE

Alfred Holt

Private, Private, lie next to me;
You know, my friend, I cannot see;
Please cover me with your brown coat;
I'm gurgling mud here, in my throat.

Young soldier, please stay by my side;
Tell my girl how I bravely died,
Not choking in this wicked field,
But ten, through Jerry's heart, I killed.

Take home my love, and my last words;
Say I was among the trees and birds,
Not the long, gaping wound so red,
Or the bullet hole that's in my head.

Private, Private, please do be kind,
Don't tell my mum that I went blind,
Say I went in blazing glory,
Killing Jerry. Make a good story.

MIDNIGHT

Ann Cooper

Well, I've settled into my new yard which is much bigger than Peartree Stables. There are two large stable blocks, one for the Mares, one for the Noballs. It means us girls can have a good gossip without having to shout across the yard. The girls tell me the Noballs like it too; they can spend the night in typical male fashion, swapping dirty jokes and holding farting competitions. I wouldn't like to be the human that has to open up their stable block in the mornings!

At the far end of the yard there are three more stables but only one is occupied.

I was a bit apprehensive when I first arrived, but the girls are very friendly. I soon felt at home as I listened avidly to all the gossip. I was warned about the occupant of the outside stables, a black stallion called Midnight. Apparently, he thinks he's God's gift to mares and tries it on with all the girls. His Human bolts his door at night, but he's learnt to get his lips round the bolt (I'm told his lip action's very good) and opens up his door. When he's feeling randy he trots down the yard, and undoes our door for a midnight visit. (Well named it seems.) He tries to tell everyone that he's the original symbol of Lloyds Bank. As if! He's too dumb to realise how old that would make him. Daft devil, he's obviously all mouth and swishing tail.

On my second day I met him face to face. He had been turned out into the field next to ours, and he spotted me straight away. Up went his tail like a flag and he galloped round his field a couple of times so I could see how fit he was. Show off! Then he came over to the fence, snorted a couple of times and started his chat up routine.

"Hiya, darlin'. You new here?" Nought out of ten for originality! "You're a pretty young thing, aren't you? A real golden girl. I love your long flaxen hair."

What did he expect? I'm a Palomino—what colour did he think I was going to be?

I answered him politely; well, you know I'm renowned for my good manners. His conversation didn't get any better, though.

"I think we're really going to hit it off. You're definitely my type. I fancy you rotten. How about I pay you a little visit tonight, sweetheart? We could get it on together. What d'ya say?"

What I wanted to say wasn't printable but I gave my opinion loud and clear. "I don't fancy you one bit and if you think you're getting your oats in *my* stable, you've got another think coming!"

With that I flashed my tail at him (no harm in him catching a glimpse of what he wasn't getting) and galloped off.

Last Tuesday we had a new girl come, name of Lily; very young and very pretty, but like all youngsters, thinks she knows it all.

That evening we all warned her about Midnight, but would she listen? She just tossed her mane muttering, "Whatever."

Next morning, sure enough, Midnight chatted her up and she spent most of the day flirting with him over the fence. Silly filly! When we returned to our stable block we tried to warn her once again, but she put on a blank expression and ignored us. What more could we do?

No one was surprised that night when Midnight came into our stable block. He used lips and teeth to open Lily's stable and she followed him out behind the barn.

No doubt he was all lovey-dovey while he led her there, but out of sight he didn't waste any time. We could hear him snorting and pawing the ground. All of a sudden the air was filled with screams; Lily was discovering that being gripped at the neck by sharp teeth while half a ton of rampant male forced himself on you wasn't the romantic encounter she'd envisaged.

When Lily started screaming, the whole yard woke up, the outside lights came on, the dogs began barking, and the Noballs were calling, trying to find out what was going on—not that they would have understood, poor things. The Governor and his missus (in her nightie!) came rushing up the yard. Midnight was furious because he'd been interrupted and was rearing, snorting and stamping on the ground. It's a wonder the Governor managed to get Lily away without getting trampled. Missus brought her back to us while the Governor struggled to get Midnight back into his stable. Lily was sobbing her little white socks off as Missus tended her cuts.

Next morning we were kept in our stable block. Midnight, however, was sent out into his field while the Governor fixed extra locks on his stable door. Bit late if you ask me. I mean, you've heard the saying, 'It's no use locking the stable door after the horse has shot his bolt!'

THE SEASHORE AT HAVERIGG

Angela Rigley

Graceful seagulls soaring
on the thermals,
Tall grasses waving
in the breeze,
White clouds scudding
across skies of blue,
soft sand and cool water
intermingling on the beach.

What delights of the seashore sights.

Gentle waves lapping,
craggy rocks creaking,
happy children giggling,
birds' wings flapping,
sand dunes sighing,
young lovers canoodling,
burly fishermen calling,
ships' horns hooting,
boats chug-chugging
through the Firth.

What scintillating sounds of the seashore.

Rain's now pelting,
Wind is howling,
Thunder's threatening.

Time to go home.

DRASTIC MEASURES

Tony Butler

George's car was already in the drive when I reached home, an unusual event as he usually worked late every night at the garage. I tried to fight down the feeling of rising irritation as I imagined him asking me to pay off yet another pressing debt. That garage of his had been a disaster from the start. He'd had one problem after another, and if it wasn't for my flourishing Country Meat Pie business he'd have gone under years ago.

I let myself in and frowned. George was talking to someone on the telephone. "....I shall have to take drastic measures. I'll take her to the cleaners."

I swear I almost had a heart attack, and had to force myself to breathe. Somehow George had found out about my affair with Alex, my golf pro.

I don't know how I found the strength to leave the kitchen and climb the stairs to our bedroom. This would finish me in this town; I'd be a laughing stock, a joke! In my mind's eye I could see my former friends laughing together, and joking about Joanne and her toy-boy. I had always tried to put the fact that my lover was only twenty-six, and just two years older than my daughter, Jessica, out of my mind.

I would also be ruined, because George would demand half the business. Half of *my* business! I would lose everything I'd worked for, including the new Judd's Pubs contract. It was a nightmare.

Unless you stop him! The voice just came into my head from nowhere. Stop him and save myself, but how?

George was in the lounge reading a newspaper when I walked in, and he actually had the nerve to look pleased to see me, the hypocrite. Oh, how I hated his smug, self-satisfied smile.

"I thought I'd finish early and spend some time with you, perhaps take you out for a meal," he said. But I could see right through him. He was trying to get me nice and relaxed, and then tell me he knew about my affair.

Well, I now had plans of my own for George, and it didn't include making him rich.

"What a lovely surprise," I said, beaming at him. "You go and get ready while I have a coffee; oh, and we'll have to call in at Country Meat Pies on the way. I forgot to post the weekend duty roster."

"All right, love, I'll go and take that bath," George said.

We pulled into the car park of the factory unit that was now Country Meat Pies, and I unlocked, deactivated the alarm and led him inside. He whistled in surprise at how much bigger the plant had grown, and showed a mechanic's interest in the machinery that I'd had installed.

The mincer could take a whole side of frozen beef. Knowing he'd want to take a closer look, I led him up onto the walkway so he could see into it. The machine was actually comprised of three sections: the hopper, the meat flayer and, finally, the mincing blades. Once the beef was in the hopper and the power was turned on, the hopper revolved at high speed, throwing the meat onto the small, round revolving blades that stripped the flesh from the bones. The bones would be removed, then the flesh lowered into the next chamber, and a hydraulic arm would push a stainless steel plate onto the flesh, forcing it through the holes in the mincing plates.

My handbag slipped out of my hand and fell with a clatter into the empty hopper and I tried to hook it out with some tongs used to remove bones.

“Hold on a second, Jo, I’ll get it for you,” George said and lowered himself into the hopper.

His screams didn’t last very long at all. I didn’t look until the mincing stopped and allowed me to remove the bones. The pulveriser soon took care of them. The crushed and powdered remnants went into the canal at the rear of the unit.

My handbag was ruined, and it took a while to remove his teeth and clothing from the mince. Fortunately, I found his rings and watch almost straightaway.

George finally made almost three dozen individual Country Meat Pies which I packed, ready for delivery.

At two am it was all over and, humming the same tune that George had, I went home to bed.

I swear I almost had a heart attack when I was awakened by Cassie, my granddaughter, jumping on my stomach.

“Stop that right now, Cassie!” Jessica, my daughter said, looking more like George than ever.

“What,” I asked, “exactly do you want, Jessica?”

“Minnie Mouse,” Jessica said and, seeing my blank look, added, “You know the Minnie Mouse backpack that Dad bought me in Disneyland when I was five? I thought Cassie might like it. I phoned Dad last night and he said that Minnie was looking a little grubby, so he’d take her to the cleaners. I thought I’d save him the bother. Mom....Mom!”

Take her to the cleaners! My chest contorted with an agonising pain. I couldn’t breathe. Jessica was looking down at me, and then everything faded away.

JOURNEYS

Annette Jones

I take a journey every day,
I go to far off lands,
To climb a mountain,
Swim a lake, or trek across the sands.

Or else I walk the city streets
In someone else's shoes.
I try out different lifestyles
To see which path I'd choose.

I travel back in time, perchance,
By charger, stagecoach, train.
I sail the seas or march to war
And then come home again.

I take a rocket into space
And visit alien stars,
To see what's in the future,
And is there life on Mars?

I live a thousand lives a year,
Detective, cowboy, queen.
I fall in love, or solve a crime;
It's such a change of scene.

I make these journeys from my bed,
Or chair or cosy nook.
Of course you've guessed my vehicle:
The pages of a book!

WHEN BOBO MET DOLLY

Shirley McIntyre

Until a few months ago, my life had been unremarkable. I lived with Keely and Karen in a small house in Nottingham. I only ever went out into the yard, and spent my days snoozing or gazing out of the window. One of the girls came home each lunchtime to let me out, and give me little strokes, and there was always food and water in the kitchen. Every few weeks Keely clipped a shiny red patent lead to my designer collar, and then we strutted down the road to 'Paws to Pamper'. There I spent a luxurious couple of hours being clipped, coiffed, cosseted, and combed.

One day, though, when we got back, the house was full, and everyone made a fuss of me. I felt like a celebrity.

"Ooh, look at him, he's too cute, Kaz! Come here, BoBo, let's take your picci."

"Thanks, mate, he's my special boy, aren't you, BoBo? I had you beautified specially for the Christmas Eve party, didn't I, my baby?"

It wasn't long before the novelty—me—wore thin. I took to my bed while the booze flowed, and the music got louder. I've never been much of a party animal, to be perfectly honest.

The next day, Christmas, was a miserable affair. Both girls and half the students from St Anns, were lolling around all over. The Christmas tree was lolling around too, its baubles squashed or broken. Some time later, after the last pasty-faced guest had left, and Keely and Karen had forced down pasta and something they referred to ominously as 'The hair of a dog', it was pressie-opening time.

I excitedly bit through sticky tape and various garish Rudolphs to reach what I'd hoped would be a bag of festive Doggie treats, at the very least. My disappointment was palpable when I saw it: a small, crimson Santa Claus outfit. Attached, was a label that boasted, 'Suitable for small Shih Tzus' and below that, an unflattering picture of an exceptionally ugly example of my breed.

Reluctantly, I allowed myself to be squashed into the embarrassing costume, then sat, lay, and rolled, as instructed, while the girls cackled and clicked their iphones.

The New Year began and my days trundled along without incident. Then, one Sunday afternoon, I was jolted from my nap by a knocking at the door. I barked and ran around like a mad thing, as you do.

When Keely opened the door, I heard, "Oh, hello. Is this him then? Is this BoBo?"

"Yes, this is BoBo. Come in." I followed everyone into the front room and fussed around the visitors' legs. The woman seemed to really like me, and the bloke said, "He does seem a nice little chap."

The deal was done and dusted in a heartbeat. Keely even threw in my red patent lead and designer collar when a sizeable amount of money exchanged hands. She even briefly stopped counting it to pat my head and say goodbye. I happily got into something called a car, jumped on the woman's knee and, without a backward glance, sped away to my new home. I felt a bit anxious and it brought on my nervous flatulence. Nobody seemed to mind, though.

This car ride was a pleasant experience, and I was just nodding off when the woman said, "BoBo, you'll be living with us from now on. I'll be your Mum and he, (pointing to the bloke) will be your Dad." I hadn't a clue what she was waffling on about. *What was a mum and dad? What was a car? What was anything on this very strange Sunday?*

Soon we were 'home' and I enthusiastically jumped out. This new mum and dad opened some gates onto grass. I've always liked grass. You don't see much grass in St Anns. Anyway, I gambolled over it like a mad thing. And then couldn't stop. The lawn went downhill and I swear my little legs were moving at a squillion miles an hour. Then splash, I was swimming! I could only manage to doggy-paddle a few strokes, and I was scared Shih-less, I don't mind telling you. Just as my life floated before me, a big strong hand grabbed my collar and hauled me up a muddy bank.

"Come on, you silly little bugger. That's given you a rude awakening hasn't it? You won't go running down there so fast again, will you? That's the stream. Ugh, you're sodden. Get a towel, Shirl."

It was great being rubbed and cuddled by Mum. I felt very safe and loved. Then I noticed her...Dolly.

Mum says Dolly is my sister. I find this surprising as we don't look anything like each other. Dolly has rough, ginger, spiky hair, whereas mine's soft, black and wavy. Whatever. Everything about this new life of mine is 'whatever'. For instance, I'm never alone. If Mum and Dad aren't here, Dolly is. Most of the time, though, I think she hates me. She's very jealous, and can be a right bitch if I try to usurp her 'top dog' status.

I just wish she'd understand I'm here to stay, and no amount of growling and scowling will alter that. I'm not some daft dope of a dog; I know when I'm on a winner.

In spite of Dolly's idiosyncrasies, I've grown to love her. I especially love sniffing round her tuppence. This is another new experience for me, and a jolly nice one it is, too. Dolly pretends not to like it, but I don't believe it. I've heard on Jeremy Kyle that girls are like that; they play hard to get.

So life's pretty good. I have free run of the house and garden, a dog flap in the door so I can come and go as I please, good varied grub (Doll says Dad was a Michelin-rated chef for canines in an earlier life, but she always exaggerates) and two walks every day. I enjoyed these outings immensely. Until that is, the introduction of the double lead. This clever innovation was invented by Dad.

"I wonder if I could get this patented?" he mused to nobody in particular.

"Ahem, I really don't think so, Rob," said my mother in a scathing voice.

Anyway, Dad's 'Dual Doggie Lead' works fine some of the time, but if Dolly is in a bad mood, you know, hormones out of sync, that time of the month, or if she's just simply sicker of me than usual, then this is when she comes into her own. There we'll be, pulling and tugging together, united in our joint effort to make Mum break into a run, when suddenly I'm nearly garrotted. Dolly stops dead in her tracks, just when I'm in full pelt. Sometimes, I grant you, this is for a genuine wee, but more often, it's just out of pure malice. The pressure nearly takes my head off, I kid you not. *Hmm, two can play at that game, there's more than one way to skin a dog. I'll have a go at that.*

Unfortunately for me my sister is much stronger than I thought, so when *I* stop suddenly while *she's* steaming along, she simply drags me after her. I've only tried it a couple of times and quickly realised I was being hoist by my own petard (or, in this case, lead) and gave it up as a bad job. Dolly, however, cottoned on to my cunning plan, so now, every time I genuinely need to stop for a wee or poo, she drags me away. Imagine that! It's so embarrassing and disgusting, especially if her mates, the Shar Peis are around. The three of them have a right giggle at my expense.

My sister, Dolly, is behaving more strangely than usual. As you're aware from my earlier musings, she's mixed breed, well, she's a mongrel, really. Oh, she pontificates about being something called a 'Brussell', pretentious or what? Hardly in the same league as Labradoodle, now, is it? But I'm afraid there's no way round it. My Sister Is A Mongrel. Anyway with such dodgy doggie genes I suppose bizarre behaviour goes with the terriertory, and we make allowances for her irrational hatred of cars, of fluffy black dogs (me in particular) and her hysterical howling when Mum and Dad go out. However, this latest quirk is something else.

Picture the scene: Mum clickety clicking knitting needles, me BoBo, snuggling up beside her, Dad watching Top Gear, and Dolly, snottily snoring, sprawled on the back of the sofa just above Mum's head. Suddenly, the mad bitch leaps down, using poor Mum's shoulder as a ladder, launches herself into the middle of the shag-pile, and rolls around like a loon on crack cocaine. Peace is shattered, chaos descends. Mum drops stitches and swears like a foul-mouthed fish wife, my back legs get ravelled up in red and white wool (Christmas is coming and so are festive doggie sweaters), Jeremy Clarkson's voice gets even louder, and daft Doll still rolls around with a dreamy, dopey smile on her face.

"Oh, I say, look at Dolls," smiles Mum adjusting her varifocals, while squinting at the tangled four-ply. "She ought to be in a circus, performing tricks like that. Come on, girl, let's see another roly-poly. Isn't she funny, Bo?"

As suddenly as it begins, the performance is over and Dolly the Daft Performing Dog, leaps back onto the sofa, using Mum's shoulder as a ladder again, and continues her snotty snoring. Over the next few nights, Doll's cabaret becomes a regular event. Even when Mum is engrossed in Coronation Street—normally a sacrosanct half hour—even that doesn't deter the barmy Brussell and her antics. She could at least wait for the adverts!

We're getting kind of bored with the floor show when Saturday comes round and it's time for our weekly grooming session while watching X Factor. Suddenly Dad interrupts the contestants' blubbering and caterwauling by shouting, "Oh, my God, what's this? And this? Oh, there's another...and another."

"Another what, another what?" shrieks Mum, dropping more stitches.

Then it all becomes clear, everything falls into place, that elusive piece of the jigsaw. MY SISTER HAS BUGS. She's infested. Lousy. However you dress it up, Dolly has fleas. Bleugh.

Sunday's chaotic. Dad hot-foots it to Pets at Home for Bob Martins anti-flea shampoo, Mum checks on the supplies of Frontline and nit combs, then it's all systems go. The scabby ginger mongrel is de-loused. As we've come to expect, when she has her bi-annual bath, she howls the place down, then shakes her scummy hairy lather all over Mum's net curtains. Worse is to come, though—the hairdryer.

It sends her into an apoplectic frenzy. She whines, squeals, rolls her eyes and dribbles. Gross. For the first time since Dolly and I have been siblings, I feel superior. Top Dog you might say.

So there we are, a few evenings later, Dad upstairs escaping Corrie, Mum frantically knitting, and Dolly snoring. Suddenly I feel it. At the bottom of my back, just near my show-off frondy tail, something's crawling. I launch myself on to the shag-pile and roll around hysterically.

Unbelievable! Me, BoBo McIntyre, a Shih Tzu with pedigree, has fleas. Dolly's dirty squatters have taken up residence in my luxurious wavy black locks.

We all feel a sense of déjà vu. Grounddog day once more...

THROUGH A CHURCH DOOR

Barrie J Kinsella

An oaken door opens on silence unbroken,
The church, a thousand years standing
In thy sight;
A timeless calm holds us enthralled.
Enchanted, we stand, absorbing the peace,
A soundless congregation
Reaching back through time.
Is all around us in transparent display?
Rays of sunshine, with gentle motes falling,
Highlights stained glass in all its glory;
Soaring arches with columns surrounding,
History interwoven, enclosed in its fabric,
Internal voices, by listening we'll hear.
Ongoing mysteries for us will appear;
Centuries of worship, heralding Christ the King.
Evensong breaks into celestial life;
sacred songs with voices uplifted,
Echoing through the ages
with the turning of pages.

GOSSAMERS ABOUND

Mike Hemstock

Geese are in season, gossamers abound,
Swaying grass makes hardly a sound;
The warmth of the sun, a cool summer breeze,
The freshness of autumn, the rustling leaves.

Lightly, zephyrs float along,
Migratory birds sing their song.
Nature's progression moving ahead,
Will they return? Will they be dead?

THE TICKING BOMB

Alfred J Holt

Mildred looked at the telegram for the millionth time. She placed it on her bedside table and walked to his side of the bed, looking intensely as if to see him there. She stooped, placed her hands on her knees, lowered her head, and kissed the pillow fervently. Tears soaked the spot where her dearest Robert had once lain.

The sirens sounded, and she heard neighbours running. "Come on, Millie, there's a dud stuck in Robson Street. It's ticking," shouted a familiar voice through her letterbox. However, she stayed with the pillow, transfixed to where her lover had slept.

Somewhere in her heart Mildred knew the siren was calling her to safety. Nevertheless, she already felt safe, her whole being secure in the knowledge she could soon be with her beloved Robert.

She shouted back, "Be down in a minute, Rube." Then, reluctantly, she pulled herself away, and walked to the living room, swigged some brandy from the bottle on the mantelpiece, went back to the bedroom and lay on the bed, cuddling the pillow.

Outside, bobbies ran around, clearing the streets, shouting through megaphones and banging on doors, until quietness indicated desertion of the doomed street.

Minutes later a deafening sound was heard and bits of once-cherished homes showered the area.

As Mildred had promised herself, she and Robert were together again.

THE OWL

Ann Cooper

Ghost wings hovering
Frenzied squeaking
Swooping
Bloodied talons
Silence

APRIL

Ann Cooper

It's softly snowing petals in the lane,
Primroses smile on the grassy bank,
Proud gold lions watch over blushing daisies,
Jack's white eyes peep from the hedgerow,
And in the woods, the first hint of dreamy blue,
Pale sun lightening my world,
Perfect April day,
Mellow harmony.
And then I turn the corner.
Rape!
Stretching into the distance,
A screaming sea of acid yellow,
Discordant, disfiguring, disastrous.
Rape of the countryside.

EXPIATION

Gordon F Butler

Duncan looked at his watch:16.25 Thursday 23-9-2004. Forty-two years to the day since it had happened, forty years to the day he had left. Somehow it felt right, returning on the anniversary of events, just as it had felt right to leave on the anniversary of the first event.

'Matlock next stop,' the speakers announced. 'This service terminates here.'

The train groaned to a halt and, with a sigh, the doors opened. Reluctantly Duncan stood, picked up his rucksack and moved onto the platform. The sign, MATLOCK, faced him. He looked all around.

'God! How it's changed,' he said out loud.

'Most things do, mate,' declared the driver, walking past. 'Depends how long it is since you've been here.'

'Too long,' Duncan replied. 'Last time I came in from Manchester.'

'Bloody hell, that was way back. Where've you been since?'

'Travelling, too long and too far. When's the last one back to Derby?'

'Half past ten, but if you're ready before that there's one at five to nine, okay?'

'Fine, thanks.'

The driver carried on and Duncan walked out of the station and along the road for Derby to the nearest pub. Ordering a pint, he sat in a corner where he could see the whole room.

Old habits die hard, he thought as he took some newspaper cuttings, yellow with age, from his rucksack and looked at the headlines.

MISSING MATLOCK GIRL. ONE WEEK AND NO SIGN. SUSPECT RELEASED. NO EVIDENCE OFFERED.

He didn't bother with the rest of the articles; he knew them off by heart. Would the place be the same? Would he recognise it? Could he even find it? Forty years is a long time.

Taking a good pull of his pint, he leant back and closed his eyes. Once more he could see her: blonde curls surrounding a pair of bright blue eyes, and cheeks red with the wind. She smiled and he smiled back.

'It'll be alright,' he reassured her. 'Not long now and everything will be fine, you'll see.'

'You okay, mate?' the barman asked as he shook Duncan's shoulder.

'Yes, fine thanks, just daydreaming out loud, that's all. Do you have any sandwiches or anything to eat? I'm starving.'

'I can do you a ham cob, if that's enough.'

'That'll be fine. Could you make it two, thanks?'

The barman left but not without taking close note of Duncan's features, particularly the pallor of his face.

'Looks like he's just out of prison,' he said to the girl leaning on the bar, as he went through to the kitchen.

Duncan took a modern OS Map out of his pocket and perused it, then compared it to a piece of a much older one, trying to commit it to memory. Satisfied, he put both maps away just in time for his rolls arriving.

'Two pound fifty, if you know what that means?'

'Should do, we've been decimal since 1971, haven't we?' Duncan retorted, handing over the money. 'Yes, I've been inside, but not in the way you think. I've been ill, but it's over. Now I'd like to eat in peace.'

'Okay, mate, no offence meant, just being friendly.'

The barman returned, muttering to the girl, 'Bloody hell, he's got ears like a bat. Be careful what you say.'

Duncan just waved at them, smiled and ate his cobs. Forty years since leaving, bumming around the world, then the last fifteen in a mental institution. Yes, he'd been inside, more than anybody could know.

After leaving the pub, he stood on the bridge, looking down at the River Derwent. In the late summer evening light the river, at least, seemed the same.

'You're coming, then?' The voice in his head began again. Closing his eyes, Duncan tried to will the voice away, but back it came. 'You're quite near, I can tell. Are you coming today?'

Duncan knew better than to try to reply. The best thing would be to fix his mind on something else. Looking around, he saw a couple in an embrace. The man's hand was sliding all over his girl friend. Watching them gave Duncan the means to quiet the voice, but stirred other feelings. Quickly he walked away up the minor road for Snitterton and the old quarries.

He realised he'd been longer in the pub than he'd intended and the light had begun to fade. He hurried, wanting to reach his goal before darkness fell. The rucksack becoming heavier with each stride, he considered dumping it. As he neared the top of the hill he stopped for a breather, leaning against the wall. The whole of Matlock spread out below, the line of the Derwent shining silver, the street lights becoming prominent.

'Did you ever see this, Susan?' he muttered to himself.

'You know I didn't,' the voice replied. 'How could I? I wasn't tall enough to see over the wall.'

'I know, I should have thought.'

Throwing the rucksack to the ground, he held his head in his hands and shouted, 'Who the hell am I talking to? They're only imaginings, they're not real. I can manage without them.'

'Can you? I'm real enough, aren't I? I know you're very near, and I'm waiting,' the voice came again.

'You can bloody well carry on waiting. I'm not coming. I'm going back.'

He picked up the rucksack and started back down the hill, but his steps faltered and he nearly fell into the road. Leaning against the wall to steady himself, he looked at his map—he could just make it out in the failing light. His goal was very near. He should complete the task. After all, he had promised.

But does a promise hold when the person promised is dead? Duncan didn't know.

To hell with it, I'll do it.

The rucksack slung over one shoulder, he carried on up the hill to the first quarry. Realising this one was on the wrong side of the road, he moved to the next. There he saw the gates as he remembered, apart than being covered with rust and warning notices.

He put the rucksack on the ground, took out his maps and a small torch. Everything fell into place. Definitely the correct gate. He took out a box and a sheet of white card in a plastic sleeve, fastened the box to the gate with some cable ties and tied the notice over it. Then he hung the rucksack from the railings and scrambled over.

'It's all right, Susan, Daddy's coming. I'm so sorry I've been so long.'

'I knew you'd come.'

'I'm here now, everything's going to be fine, I promise.'

A milkman on his early round found the note the next morning and called the police.

The box contained the birth certificate of Susan Harrison who had gone missing in 1962 and had never been found. The note quite simply said,

I, Duncan Harrison, the father of Susan, knew my brother, Malcolm Harrison, killed her, but couldn't prove anything. I promised to avenge Susan, and now all our living relatives are dead I have done so. I have killed my brother; you will find his body at his home. My body is at the bottom of the quarry where you should also find the remains of Susan. May we all rest in peace.

'Amen,' said the policeman on reading it.

GLOBAL WARMING

Barrie J Kinsella

I had a dream
That I had saved the world
From global warming.
The hero of the hour was I.
Polar bears saluted me as we passed
On the snow-clad streets,
Penguins flapped their flippers in accord.
Ice frosted the bleak landscape
As the snow ploughs came by
In never ending convoys.
The Nobel Peace Prize
Was mine for the taking,
For how could crime flourish
In temperatures
Far below the freezing limits?
You may ask how I achieved
This miracle of nature.
I will only smile and assure you
It's me to know
And you to find out.
My legacy is ongoing
And will benefit all mankind
As long as the sun rises
In the morning and sets in the evening
Underneath our polar skies.

ODE TO A REFEREE

Mike Hemstock

This is the tale of a day in the life
Of an ordinary man, with two kids and a wife;
But like a werewolf changes, so does he,
When at weekends he becomes a Football Referee.

We believe that a ref is a curious breed.
He has to be, because the players, they need
Someone to shout at, to rant at, and rave.
The referee must also be daring and brave.

He has to put up with a whole lot of stick,
And everyone reckons that 'He is thick'.
The referee's back is as broad as a barn,
As many a player spins him a yarn.

'His parents aren't married.' 'He's totally blind.'
'Nobody loves him.' 'He's out of his mind.'
'Get a move on, Ref, and keep up with play.'
These are the things the players may say.

He arrives at the ground in plenty of time;
The lines aren't marked out (they've ran out of lime).
He's checking the nets and inspecting the flags,
When the secretary comes along, carrying the bags.

Back at the pavilion the home team arrive,
Then the opponents, but, hey, there are only five.
"Where are the others?" the secretary asks;
Just another one of his menial tasks.

"They'll be here in a minute," says a spotty young lad.
"They've just gone to pick up somebody's dad."
"It can't be the ref's," says a fan who is plastered,
"He hasn't got one, because he's a b*****d."

The kick off time approaches so fast,
They've actually sent him assistants, at last.
Looking like penguins in black and white suits,
Black and white socks and black and white boots.

Toss of the coin for 'Choice of Ends',
Shake of the hands to say, 'We are Friends',
Blow the whistle to start the game,
All hell's let loose, and who is to blame?

Who'd be a ref now in this day and age,
When all players act as if they're on stage?
Is it a penalty or maybe it's not,
When a player goes down, near the penalty spot?

"Aw, come on, Ref, now do get a grip,
That was a kick, if it wasn't a trip."
And when the attacker happens to fall,
"Flipping 'eck, Ref, I went for the ball."

You will often hear the players all shout,
"Our ball, Ref!" as one kicks it out.
And then, when he spots the offside trap,
A cheeky defender gives him a clap.

When he thinks the game has been mastered,
Some person calls him a stupid b*****d.
He'll have to reply, although it is hard,
By showing the player the famous Red Card.

On the day that they play a big cup game,
When some players kick, clog, and maim,
I sometimes think (though I never do say it),
I'd rather officiate than actually play it.

To sum it all up in a wry sort of a way,
The referee's someone who'd much rather play,
But because of an injury or just lack of skill,
He takes to the whistle. It just fits the bill.

In spite of the trouble, the hassle and abuse,
The referee thinks he can be of some use.
He isn't a weakling; in fact he's quite strong,
And he is as honest as the day is long.

He does his job without complaining,
Whether it's cold or whether it's raining.
At the end of a day full of trouble and strife,
He returns to his family (two kids and a wife).

A DIFFERENT VIEW

Dawn Raffle

Davy watched his parents disappear into the crowd of jostling holiday makers; a light touch on his arm reminded him he was lumbered with Gran.

"They won't be long, Davy, just need some time on their own..." Her voice trailed off.

He didn't answer, resentment choking any reply. He hadn't wanted to come on the club outing to Blackpool, with good reason. Dad had brought Gran, wheel-chair and all, and Davy knew he'd be the one stuck with her. He was too young, at thirteen, to stay at home on his own, but old enough to take care of Grandma. It wasn't fair.

"Davy, lets go for a cup of tea. You can have an ice cream." Gran looked at him expectantly, the annoyance on his face plain to see. She sighed. He reminded her of his grandfather when put out, his jaw jutting out, stubbornly hiding his feelings from the world. She wished she had stayed at home. The last thing she wanted was to spoil Davy's day. They should have taken him with them. She'd have been okay sitting watching the sea, but her protests had fallen on deaf ears.

"Okay," he answered and pushed her wheelchair towards the refreshment kiosk, parking it near the sea wall, and reluctantly joining the queue. Wistfully, he looked at the double flakes and raspberry ripples. No chance; she'd given him just enough for tea and a small ice-cream. Glancing back to see if she was alright, he was irritated to see her looking miserable. Why didn't she take her coat off? She must be red hot, and why had she come? It was obvious she wasn't enjoying herself. He looked longingly back at the fairground. Even if he could go, he had no money.

Slowly, he walked back with her tea. "Here you are, Gran."

She smiled and took her tea. "Thanks, Davy."

A loud 'Yoo hoo', accompanied by a guffaw, caused Gran to tut. Mrs Dawson, club secretary, grinning from ear to ear, plonked herself on the wall next to her. "Hello, Clara, how are you?" she trilled. Before Gran could answer she continued, "Davy grows each time I see him. Them trousers can't stand much more taking down. Still, he's a good boy. Not many thirteen-year olds would spend time looking after their grandma while Mum and Dad were in the pub. They're not daft bringing you, lad, and keeping right side of your Gran as well."

Davy, watching the bobble of spit on her lip, moved Gran out of range. Gran shot him a grateful look, which changed to one of relief as Mrs Dawson stood up and said, "Got to go. I'm meeting Fred in the bookies. Nice talking to you. Ta- ta."

She waddled away, her dress straining over her rear end, and her pull-up knee-highs creating a new line in ankle socks.

Gran murmured, "Nice talking to you, too."

Davy noticed the sarcasm in her voice, and realised Mrs Dawson had never even looked at Gran when she had spoken to her, or given her chance to speak. Maybe that was why Gran was miserable: 'cos no one listened to her.

"Davy, I'm fed up with this, but as I'm lumbered with you, I might as well make the best of it. Let's go somewhere where we can enjoy ourselves."

He stared at her stern face. His heart sank as visions of the duck pond in the park filled his mind. "What do you want to do, Gran?"

Her mouth creased into a smile, and her eyes twinkled. "Do you fancy Blackpool tower?"

"Blackpool tower? What about the wheelchair?"

"We'll use the lifts, but if you don't want to go..."

The Tower was great. Lifts took them to the top, and Gran enjoyed seeing the ballroom again. She told him stories about his Granddad, and some of the crazy escapades he'd got up to. At first, Davy listened because he felt he had to, but then he found himself enjoying it, laughing along with her. Afterwards, they went onto the crazy golf course. Gran even took her coat off, and with Davy helping her, she managed a paddle in the sea, laughing when a wave splashed her.

"How about another ice cream before we go on the funfair?" Gran said, her face flushed, and perspiration running down her face.

"Are you alright, Gran?"

"Never better, son."

"Cheers, Gran." The day was turning out okay.

Gran watched him ride on the dodgems, waving and smiling as he went past.

They had just reached the big wheel when Dad and Mum caught up with them. "We thought you'd be on the park." Mum looked guiltily at Davy. "Sorry, son, we met some old friends in the welfare and time just passed."

"We were just about to go on the big wheel," Gran said, surprising them all. Whether it was the assumption of her sitting on the park that had made her decide to chance it, Davy could only guess, and Gran was determined, despite their protests. She was going to ride on the big wheel.

All the way up Gran rigidly gripped the safety bar, her eyes closed tightly. At the top, the wheel stopped, and a soft cool breeze stirred her hair.

Davy touched her gently. "Gran, look."

She opened her eyes and, looking around, smiled.

The town spread out like a colourful map beneath them, a carpet of houses and buildings, stretching for miles, with different shapes and sizes, and rows of office blocks, dwarfing church steeples; roads with parks nearby, bringing touches of green amongst the brick and concrete.

The tower stood king of all. It dominated the promenade, overlooking trams and buses filled with holidaymakers, a continuous stream winding along congested roads. Sunlight dappled on the grey sea, and laughing children jumped in the waves. Families played, while donkeys patiently walked the sands. Men fished on the pier, and ships sailed on the horizon to unknown destinations.

"It's grand," Gran said softly, her careworn face animated, her blue eyes shining with unshed tears. She looked younger, enjoying every magical moment.

Davy's eyes brimmed; he'd never seen Gran like this.

The wheel moved, descending to the mortal realm. Sounds of laughter and screams of excitement filled the air. Music competed with voices, vendors selling their goods amidst thousands of conversations, a melody of humanity. Smells of fish and chips, hotdogs, onions and doughnuts reminded Davy he was hungry.

Dad helped Gran off the wheel. "Come on, Mum." Shaking his head, he grinned. "I don't know, at your age. You'll be paddling in the sea next."

Gran just smiled.

Davy started to speak but caught the look in Gran's eyes. Seeing the twinkle, he understood and learned. Some things are best left unspoken.

THE WILLOW

Ann Cooper

The neighbours stood gossiping over the wall,
Surveying the willow that had grown so tall.
"Now, you all know as I'm not one to complain,
But what if them roots grow into me drain?"
"I'm the one wiv a grievance, beggin' your pardon,
Look how that tree blocks the light from me garden;
Leaves make it slippy where the kids want to play,
And I can't see them houses over the way."
Then, one weekend, everyone's peace was shattered
As into the garden two workmen clattered.
Their chainsaws ended king willow's long reign,
It fell, conquered—ignominiously slain.
Summer came and the hot sun blazed on and on,
But there was no respite, for the shade had gone.
The neighbours chuntered, "Why couldn't they let be?"
"What made them chop down that lovely old tree?"
"You know it's not like me to keep bitchin',
But them at the back now look straight in me kitchen.
These gardens now all look empty and bare.
Them's what chopped it down just don't seem to care."
One Autumn day the neighbours' wish was granted;
In place of the willow, a sapling was planted.
Time passed and it grew to a tall leafy plane.
"Now you all know as I'm not one to complain …"

BOZZIE'S NEW LIFE

Dianne Rasmussen

Bozzie hadn't been feeling well for several weeks but, that day, he felt he could face life no more. He went out through the cat door and settled down in his favourite place under the acer bush and closed his eyes, hoping he would fall asleep and not wake up again.

Drifting in and out of sleep, he heard her call, "Bozzie, Bozzie." He tried to ignore her but the voice became more plaintive. "Bozzie, where are you? Please, Bozzie, come home." Unable to resist the sadness in his beloved mistress's words, even though pain racked his body, he raised himself up and limped to the door. The pain increased when she picked him up, but it was good to relax against her warm body as she stroked him.

"Poor Bozzie," she said as she smoothed her hand gently along his now slightly-matted, long fur. "You've had enough, haven't you?" She took him into the lounge, laid him gently on the sofa, and turned to her partner. "I'll have to take him to the vet to end his life quickly. We can't let him suffer any more." A sob caught in her throat and gave way to a few tears, before she went out to phone the vet and prepare the cat basket. His birth sister, Tiggy, watched curiously.

Bozzie hardly woke when he was put into the cat basket, or when the vet looked him over before giving him an injection which relaxed him totally into a deep sleep. He was not aware when he was buried under the acer bush, and he didn't hear the sad goodbyes from Tiggie and his human friends. It seemed a long time before he began to surface. *It could have been hours, even days,* he thought.

His surroundings didn't seem familiar. *Maybe I'm at the vet's. Perhaps I've had an operation.* He couldn't feel the pain any more, and that made him want to smile. This increased as he remembered how his mistress had once laughed, saying, "You've got a lopsided moustache, Bozzie, but I love you, anyway."

He tried to straighten his whiskers with his face muscles but they would not move. *It must be the long sleep, and that's why I can't feel myself, or what I'm lying on.* He wanted to turn over and, even though he didn't feel the movement, he became aware of a different view of grass covered by pretty, lemon flowers.

Oh, this is odd. I'll close my eyes and, maybe, when I open them again, it will all be different. Then he realised he couldn't close his eyes but could change what he was seeing. Around him was a garden with flowering bushes, and he felt comfortable.

This is just the sort of place to relax and have a long sleep, he thought, *but I don't think I can. What's happened? Why can't I feel or see or hear anything?* He began to feel panicky. *I used to go to sleep when I wanted to work things out, but I can't, so what am I to do?*

It seemed a long time just doing nothing and trying to sort out what was happening, then, into his mind came a silver tabby cat. "You're dead, Bozzie. You can only live in your mind now and in the world as a spirit or spectre. It's a bit odd at first, but you'll get used to it."

"Is that you, Purdie?" He stopped himself, feeling a bit silly, when he know he couldn't talk to someone who couldn't be there. He was probably thinking of her because she was the mother figure that he and Tiggie had had when they'd first moved from their birth place.

"Yes, it's me, Bozzie. I'm as here as you are and, as long as you want me to read your thoughts, we can converse like this. Now what do you want to know?"

A WOMAN

Alfred J Holt

Why can’t a man be more like a woman?
There's nothing the sexes now have in common;
They snore and they fart and make such a fuss.
Oh, why can’t the males be more like us?

With wagging sharp tongues we natter all day,
And then we shoo door-to-door sellers away.
We can rustle up food in a trice on a whim,
And scrub the bath clean while singing a hymn.

Painting our nails while perched on the loo,
We can rattle to friends on our mobile phone, too!
If we stub a toe we would think nothing of it,
But men are such cissies; they curse and they spit.

We can cut down the daises and varnish the shed,
Make sure the cat, dog and kids are all fed,
Mow the front lawn and then pull up tough weeds,
Clean out the basement and sow flower seeds.

Sweep out the chimney and hose down the car,
Drive into town for a refreshing spa,
Come back and make bloomin’ family dinner,
Go to the gym to become fit and thinner.

So worn out and exhausted now do I feel,
And I’ve still got tomorrow’s damned taters to peel!
At last day is done, I sit down with a can.
I tell you, how I wish that I was a man.

THE ODD COUPLE

Barrie J Kinsella

It was a very small park, a small oasis set like a gem in the heart of London's traffic, just large enough to contain two seats facing each other across an immaculately-tended flower bed. Every weekday in summer, Dorothy sat eating her sandwiches, absorbing the calm, ordered atmosphere, a thousand miles away from the incessant demands of her increasingly-vague mother. These brief respites were thanks to the fact that her mother had developed the habit of falling into a deep sleep, lasting over an hour, after lunch.

So, there she sat, enjoying her small taste of freedom. This time it was different, though. The seat across from her was occupied by two ladies, discussing knitting, in voices that carried clearly. Then a man walked briskly into the park, surveyed the situation and asked Dorothy politely if he could sit next to her. Unaccustomed to strangers talking to her, she was barely able to nod an agreement.

Like her, the stranger unwrapped sandwiches for his lunch. "It's a lovely park, isn't it?" he remarked. "I've known about it for years and now I've moved jobs, I'll be coming here regularly."

Dorothy also agreed on the attractiveness of the surroundings, then buried her head in a newspaper. Although she could not focus on the printed words, she was very conscious of the man beside her. A hurried glance, when he had sat down, had established that he was approximately her age—forty something, tall, dark, with a pleasant manner.

Earlier than usual, she rose from the seat and walked away, followed by the man's cheery "bye".

And so a pattern developed. Most days she would arrive first, followed shortly afterwards by Ian—he'd introduced himself on their second meeting. He never talked about his home life and, too shy to ask any leading questions, she was content to share one hour with him most days. How miserable she felt when rain beat down, and she could only look out of the flat's windows, praying for it to stop. For Dorothy was in love. She admitted it to herself in the diary she kept day by day. She had never been in love before. Her opportunities were, to say the least, limited, owing to the demands her mother made on her time.

Gradually, meeting Ian every day took over her life. She dressed more carefully, spent time on her appearance, which she'd never done before. Ian, probably oblivious to her efforts to be more attractive, continued to entertain her with his easy conversation on countries visited, and experiences he'd had.

Highlights appeared in their meetings, like the first time their hands brushed when he insisted on sharing a cake, and the bliss, looking directly into his slightly-amused brown eyes when she stammered her thanks; and the supporting hand on her elbow when she stumbled, arising from the seat, one day. Moments to savour and remember.

Spring turned to summer, summer to autumn, and it soon became too cold to linger in parks. Ian had the answer. "Let's meet in the Mikado Coffee Shop only five minutes from here." Gratefully, she agreed.

Strangely, she still didn't know anything about him, nor did she want to. Dorothy was happy in the day-to-day meetings. They had discovered a mutual appreciation of art, discussing the relative merits of both old and new masters. Ian collected old prints.

One day, on an impulse, he invited her to view them. Dorothy's joy knew no bounds, a milestone in their friendship. Although difficult to arrange, she managed, at last, to arrange for Miss Humphries to sit with her mother while she went.

"Now, mind, don't be late back," was Miss Humphries parting admonishment as she left. Dorothy hardly heard, her heart singing, her footsteps light, as she made her way across London on the tube train.

Ian also lived in a flat, much smarter than Dorothy's, and beautifully furnished. The prints were first class, obviously expensive. While he was pointing out a particular detail, the sound of a key in the door was followed by the entrance of a young man in fashionable black trousers and hand-embroidered yellow shirt.

"Dorothy, this is Paul," explained Ian, "my partner."

Dorothy froze. The world stopped, and then crashed about her ears. Dimly, she heard herself talking to Paul, what about, she was never able to remember, but Paul impatiently turned on his heel, making for the kitchen, by the sounds of crockery and the singing of a kettle.

Dorothy looked at her watch, "Is that the time?" she managed to say. "Mother will wonder where I've got to."

Ian sounded disappointed. "You've only seen half the prints," he said petulantly.

Somehow Dorothy managed to make it home. The world was suddenly a grey, hard place, without joy. That was the last time she saw Ian. No sandwiches in the park, no visits to the tea shop. She had come face to face with herself, seeing a frustrated old maid, building impossible hopes on innocent chance acquaintances.

She often weeps silently on what might have been, but never could be.

GHOST

Tony Butler

I didn't wake up screaming and frantically looking around me with terror-filled eyes. In fact I just didn't wake up, period, or even possess eyes, anymore. My crumpled body lay sprawled on the ground, about fifteen feet below the spot where I kind of floated, looking down at it.

Take it from me, it was a terrible shock, not waking up, and realising I was dead. I admit I hovered, gawking in shocked disbelief at my corpse like a little kid, instead of a thirty-seven-year old ghost, spirit, or whatever the hell I was.

Then, the man who'd shot me walked over and kicked my corpse. 'You should have listened to Zoe, you piece of garbage,' he said. 'She warned you what would happen if ever you tried to replace her with a younger model.'

I found myself wondering just who this ugly, fat b*****d was. As far as I could recall, I'd never seen him until a few seconds before, when he had emerged from the shadows holding a silenced automatic, and had started pumping bullets into me. I had just slipped my metal float and hook box inside my coat and then '"bam" "bam" "bam", I was dead.

'Is...is he dead?' A woman with peroxide-bleached hair, and wearing a fun-fur coat, appeared and stood beside the gunman.

'Yeah, he's dead meat. You got the rest of my money?'

'Yes, but hadn't we better...?' She broke off and looked at my body for the first time. 'Who is this man?' she asked.

'Whatcha mean who...?' the fat man started to ask, but then a look of comprehension slowly flitted across his face, and he stared from her to my body. 'What's going on, Mrs Harris?' he asked. 'That's not your husband, is it? So who the hell is he, and why did he show up instead of Eddy?'

'Because I was doing some night fishing, you stupid moron!' I screamed, but I no longer had a voice, and he didn't even give me a second glance.

'I don't know who he is. I've never seen him before.' She looked around her nervously. 'We'd better get out of here.'

However, I knew that at that time of the morning you didn't get many people hanging around in the car-park, down there by the river. The other anglers preferred to fish a little further down, from under the trees.

'We need to get rid of his body, first,' fat-man said. 'You take off, and I'll dump him in the river.'

'Yes, okay.' She sounded relieved. 'I'd better go home in case Eddy's been trying to get hold of me. I'll call you tomorrow, George.'

'Hey, but what about my money?'

'Tomorrow, and anyway, Eddy's not dead yet.' She hurried away and I heard a car door open and then the engine fired. The headlights of her car swept in an arc, briefly illuminating my killer and my body before it drove away.

It was only when George grabbed the ankles of my corpse and started to drag it towards the river that I truly realised I really was dead. I launched myself at him.

If you've ever seen those films where ghosts melt through walls and people, well, that didn't happen. Oh, I passed inside him, all right, but that's where I stopped—inside him. It felt a lot like being inside my own body.

George, shocked by my invasion of him, released my corpse, which rolled down into the river.

'What the...?' George said, clasping his head in his hands.

'You killed me, you...you moron,' I said. 'You bloody well killed me!'

'Get out of my head,' he cried.

'No way. Where am I supposed to go?'

'I'm warning you...'

I laughed then, cutting him off in mid-flow. 'Oh, yeah! What are you going to do? Blow your own head off?'

'I suppose not,' George said, eventually, after he'd thought about it, and believe me, George was an extremely slow thinker. 'All right, what do you want? To kill me, or what?'

'That wouldn't be very clever, would it? If you die I won't have anywhere to go. You've just got rid of my body and so, as I can't have it back, I think I'd better stay put—in here with you.'

'Oh, no, you're not. I'm going to St Mary's, to see Father O'Hallion, and get you exercised.'

'It's exorcised, moron. I don't need exercising. I won't be fit for anything ever again, now, because of you.'

'Tough titty. Father O'Hallion will get rid of you for good.'

'Not so fast, George,' I said quickly. I wasn't sure that I could be exorcised, but why risk it? 'Let's talk about this, okay? Hasn't anyone ever told you that two heads are better than one?' I could almost feel his brow furrowing in concentration, and after a moment or two he nodded.

'Yeah,' he said, and nodded faster, like one of those dumb toy dogs that you see in rear car windows. 'I think it was back in reform school. "Two heads are better than none," they said. Yeah, I remember that now.'

'Well, that's what you've got. Two heads, your own head and mine. We could have a great time, George. We could even be friends.'

'Friends?' He smiled and then nodded. 'That would be okay. I don't have many friends. We'd better go back to my place, then, and sort something out. What's your name?'

'Robert. I wish I could say I was pleased to meet you.'

'Listen, Bob. I didn't mean to shoot you. It was an accident...'

'Accident!' I screamed. 'You don't walk up to someone and gun them down by accident.'

'Well, I thought you were Eddy Harris.'

'Who the hell's Eddy Harris?'

'Zoe's husband. She's paying me ten grand to kill him. I've never done this before, but I need the money to pay off Sharky Flynn. I owe him two grand, plus interest, and I only have one day left to find the money. So, when Zoe offered me this job...'

'How well do you know her?' A suspicion had occurred to me.

'Zoe's one of Sharky's hookers. Why?'

'Eddy's her husband?' If I'd been in my own body I'd have felt cold all of a sudden.

'Yeah, I already told you that. I arranged to meet Eddy here. Zoe had it all planned out.'

'What time? What time did you arrange to meet him?' I asked, raising my non-existent arm to look at my watch, which was, I remembered, now drifting down the river with my corpse.

'About now. Why?'

'You've been set up,' I said. 'If I were you I'd jump in your car and drive away from here.'

He looked shocked. 'Zoe? Set me up?' He shook his head in disbelief. 'No, not Zoe.'

As if on cue, two cars with their lights and engines turned off, coasted to a stop beside us. Eight big men piled out of the cars, their silenced automatics all pointing at George. A shrewd-looking guy, slightly slimmer and smaller than the rest, prodded a forefinger into George's chest.

'So you 'ain't got Sharkey's money, right, George? Well, you was warned, wise guy. What's gonna happen is, we're gonna take you to this place we know and make you a nice new pair of concrete boots. You're going into the river, but for good, unless you can come up with the money right now.'

Before George, who was now trembling with fear, could reply, an ambulance with siren blaring and light flashing screeched onto the jetty, followed by three police patrol cars.

Eight automatic pistols vanished from sight.

'Over here!' some one shouted. A man, wearing fishermen's waders, dragged a body out of the river—my body!

The guy who had spoken to George took hold of his arm and began leading him towards one of the cars. Paramedics were already working on my corpse.

Something tugged at me.

'Hey, do any of you know this guy?' Two cops walked towards us.

The tug came again but more insistent this time.

'George,' I hissed urgently. 'Tell them you're my brother.'

Then I was out of George and rushing into my own body's open mouth. Something belted me in the chest and I groaned.

‘He’s breathing,’ someone yelled.

I was in the ambulance before I managed to force my eyes open. George sat, looking across at me, and he smiled.

‘You were lucky,’ he said. ‘Apparently, all the bullets were stopped by that bait box you’d tucked inside your coat. The impact stopped you breathing.’

‘Yes, your brother’s right,’ one of the paramedics said, nodding in agreement. ‘I don’t know what this world’s coming to, shooting someone for kicks.’

‘Hey, George,’ I whispered hoarsely, while the paramedics were filling in their forms. ‘Are we still…you know…like…friends?’

His face lit up and, smiling like an idiot, he reached out and patted my arm. ‘Sure, we are, Bob. You betcha life we are, buddy.’

NEW BABY

Angela Rigley

They looked down, with tears in their eyes, at the tiny bundle wrapped in a blue blanket. "Our own baby boy! Can you believe it?"

"It still hasn't sunk in yet. But he was worth all that hard work and effort, wasn't he?"

"Of course he was. He's absolutely gorgeous."

"Shall we call him after my dad or yours? I think he looks more like a David than a Dennis, don't you?"

The baby stirred and stretched a foot out of the blanket.

"With those big feet and hands he looks more like a Goliath!"

"Ah, don't say that! You'll give him a complex!"

"Let's call him Daniel, then he should be able to defeat any adversary, even lions."

"Yes…Daniel…I like that."

The sleeping infant murmured as if in agreement, while his doting parents continued to gaze at him in awe.

"I was becoming quite worried at one time that I wasn't going to be able to cope, you know, when the contractions reached their worst."

"Yes, darling, but I had every faith in you. You were marvellous!"

"Didn't half make me sweat. But I did do well, didn't I? He's so lovely."

"Sweetheart, I couldn't be more proud of you."

"There wasn't as much blood as I expected, though."

"Well, dearest, darling, George, from where you were standing, wiping my brow and squeezing my hand, there wouldn't have been much blood to see."

NORTHERN LIGHTS

Ann Cooper

Panoramic firework display,
Stage-managed by ice giants,
Lights up the Arctic night,
Kaleidoscope of changing colour,
Holy radiance in the sky,
Holds me in thrall,
Transports the mind,
Uplifts the soul,
And then, like my hopes and dreams,
The colours fade and die,
Leaving nothing but the lonely cold
And Stygian darkness.

SWEET AND SOUR

David Brailsford

Fred Salt and Elsie Sugar lived together and seemed to get on fairly well, even though their personalities were so very different.

What was Elsie like? SWEET... NICE... PLEASANT... APPEALING and a real DARLING.

What about Fred? He was TART... SOUR... BITTER... UNAPPEALING... DIFFICULT and really GRUMPY.

One day Fred mislaid something and was stomping and swearing around the house. "Why can't that woman leave my things alone? She's always moving them so I can't find them."

"I don't know to what you're referring," said Elsie, so sweetly.

"There you go again, denying what you do," said Mr Salt angrily. "You'd better leave. I've had enough of you and your ways."

Because she was so NICE, she just packed a bag and left.

Of course, Mr Salt regretted her leaving but being so STUBBORN, he could not allow himself to follow after her.

As Mrs Sugar walked along, it began to rain. What would happen to Sugar if she got wet?

She would dissolve away, wouldn't she now?

She had to find shelter, didn't she?

On a hillside, she saw a house that looked like an upside-down sugar bowl, with a little door in the side. She quickly entered, to shelter from the rain.

Back with Fred, things were looking bad. The rain was dissolving the house of salt and flooding the floor.

The walls began to collapse and he had to dash outside, where things became even worse. The rain started to dissolve him, too, so he ran as fast as he could, until he came upon the sugar bowl house.

"Please let me in. The rain is washing me away."

In spite of Fred being so UNKIND, Elsie was never UNPLEASANT, so she opened the door and let him in.

She dried him with a warm towel but, as would be expected, he never said thank you.

Even so, she put her arms around him and gave him a big hug. As they hugged, their lips met in a kiss. They were still wet, so their lips stuck together.

When they managed to separate, some sweet and sour had been exchanged.

When Mr Salt next became upset about things being moved, as ANGRY words were about to pass through his lips, they brushed over sweet sugar, so he changed them. "My dear Elsie, would you know where I left my pipe? It's not in its usual place."

Mrs Sugar was just about to apologise but the words passed her sour lips, so she said instead, "I've not the faintest idea where it is. You'll have to find it yourself."

So you would think they would not be happy together... BUT THEY WERE.

They had both come to understand each other.

They lived happily ever after.

THE MEETING

Gordon F Butler

Dan was half asleep in his chair, the television providing a backdrop to his snoozing. The sound of the telephone brought him back to reality and, getting up to answer it, he saw the snow falling heavily and beginning to settle.

"Hello, Dan Shaw here," he mumbled, his voice still muffled with sleep. "Who's speaking?"

"Is that the Dan Shaw who married Elaine Breaston?" a quiet, cultured voice enquired.

"Who's speaking?" Dan asked again, now fully awake.

"Don't you recognise my voice? You should do. We were best friends for years, right through uni and for several years after."

Dan's brow furrowed with puzzlement then enlighten came, and with it trepidation. Cautiously, he spoke. "Is that Eric, Eric Marchmant?"

"You've got it, old buddy." The voice sounded lighter and more friendly. "If you can remember me I've obviously got the correct Dan."

"I can't think what you might want," Dan answered slowly, choosing his words carefully, their last meeting very fresh in his mind. "The last time we were together you threatened to knock me into the middle of the next week."

"So I did, but that was a long time ago. How many years is it? It must be twenty five, at least."

Without hesitation, Dan answered, "Twenty seven."

"My God, is it really? Doesn't time fly? I didn't know you'd come back to the village until I started trying to find you."

"Why would you be looking for me? We parted on bad terms."

Eric laughed quietly. "Oh, that's long in the past. I got over the loss of Elaine very soon. I met Helen, and Elaine disappeared into the realms of memory and what might have been. We will be having our silver wedding in a couple of months. You must come."

"Why would you want me there? Surely it would only rake up old sores?"

"I've told you, Dan, there are no sores. There can't be, can there?"

Dan didn't answer immediately. There was something in the tone of voice that made him stop and think.

"I'm sorry, Dan, I seem to have misled you." Eric's voice was carefully modulated. "I know Elaine died. I saw the headstone in the church yard. That was how I knew you'd returned. Helen and I moved into the village two weeks ago and we've been getting established. You've no idea how great it is to find out that someone you know is here already. Point of contact, you know."

"Yes, it was a blow," Dan replied softly. "It was so sudden, but I'm beginning to adjust, thank you. Now what did you really call me for?"

"Come on, don't be like that. I was doing some research into the history of the area, and I found out something about the standing stone. What did we call it? The lonely lady?"

In spite of himself, Dan laughed. "No, it was 'the last virgin', as she was the only one left standing."

"Look," Eric continued, "there's something I want to show you. Meet me there tomorrow afternoon just before four o'clock, will you?"

"Why the afternoon? It will be getting dark by then." Dan shivered.

"I know. It has to be then because of the angle of the light; any other time and it doesn't show."

Dan's curiosity was aroused and, without thinking, he agreed. "See you there tomorrow, then." He returned to his chair and to his snooze.

The lane led on, looking even gloomier under the archway of trees up ahead. Dan stumbled on, feet slipping and sliding on the newly-fallen snow.

Taking his gloves off, he reached into his great coat and took out his pocket watch. "Half past three, it'll be dark soon," he muttered to himself. "Mustn't be late. I promised him I'd be there."

Once under the trees, where the snow had yet to reach, Dan lengthened his stride, moving quickly forward. As he reached the end of the tunnel of trees he realised how dark it had become. Straining his eyes, he could just make out the silhouette of a solitary stone at the top of the hill: his goal.

Out in the open, with the snow crunchy underfoot, Dan made good speed up the final slope.

Panting slightly, he thought, *I still can't think why Eric wants to meet here when his house is in the village. We could have met there. I know what he said, but the light won't be strong enough to show anything.*

Reaching the stone, he saw a tall post stuck in the ground, about a yard away from it.

"What on earth is that doing there?" he asked openly.

"You'll never know," Eric's voice came from behind him.

The next morning, local children found a large snowman standing on top of the hill.

A couple of weeks later, when the snow melted, Dan's body was found tied to the post. A note around his neck said, 'Revenge is a dish best served cold.'

REALISATION

Barrie J Kinsella

Like a lifeboat on a troubled sea
I'll always feel safe
In the harbour of your presence.
I know you not at all
And yet, and yet
Our eyes met,
Conversation flowed.
You know everything about me,
Your perceptive glance
Reaching into my very soul.
Continue our meetings, if you please,
And I'll make thee
As happy as can be.

BICYCLE

Annette Jones

Euphemia gazed longingly at the bicycle advertisement she had sent for. She had tried to look casual, even bored, when she had taken the envelope from the silver tray proffered to her by the footman at breakfast, so as not to alert parental attention. It was an unnecessary precaution as Pater had never glanced above his paper and Mater, as usual, had given all her attention to Augustus.

Now she was safely in her room, she could dream. From her window seat she had a commanding view of the park. In the past two years it had been both a comfort and a torment, emphasising as it did, her lack of freedom to roam its beloved reaches as she had done as a child. Now she was told it was unladylike.

Instead of running wild with her brother, she had to sit and sew delicate fancy work. If she was lucky, there might be a carriage ride, or a visit, or she might take a slow constitutional stroll around the gardens with Mater.

It was all so slow!

On a bicycle she would be able to fly along the drive, out the gates and down the lanes to freedom.

Lost in this fantasy, she barely had time to stuff the brochure under a lace-trimmed pillow as her mother knocked on the door and entered. She never waited for a response.

'What was that, dear?'

'Nothing, Mama. Whatever do you mean?'

'That paper you hid. Do not imagine I failed to notice. My eyes are not yet dim with age. I hope it is not a love letter.'

'A love letter? Who could that possibly be from, Mama? I have not been allowed to meet anyone eligible yet.'

'You are too young, as you well know.'

'Too young for society, yet too old for childish things,' she sighed.

'Now, Euphemia, try not to be difficult. If you have such a nostalgia for childish things, why not take Augustus to feed an apple to his pony? But make sure your dress stays clean, please. Remember we have the vicar's wife and daughter calling for tea later.'

'Very well, Mama.'

She waited for her mother to leave, so she could continue to examine the leaflet, but Mater just stood there, frowning. 'What are you waiting for, Phemie?'

Euphemia could not defy her mother, so she left, reluctantly.

When she returned to her room and eagerly rummaged among the many frilly cushions she had made, through boredom, to decorate her window seat, the brochure was not to be found. She searched inside every pillow and peered down the back of the seat. She rang her bell and asked the maid, who had not seen it, but would go and ask the housemaid, if Miss Euphemia would wait. Yes, she would wait, but it was to no avail. On her return, the maid told her none of the servants knew anything of a brochure. After she had left, Phemie flung herself on her bed and wept in sheer frustration.

That afternoon she sat in the parlour with her mother, embroidering another useless gift. She had sufficient for three Christmases hence, yet what else was she to do?

The ladies who ran the bazaar had gently suggested to her that she had donated more than enough, and every surface in the house was covered already, several things in more than one layer. Doilies upon doilies. Sometimes she feared they would drown in doilies.

She glanced out of the window and saw a wondrous sight. Sailing with dignity up the drive were two ladies on bicycles. One saw her and waved. It was Patricia, the vicar's daughter. The other cyclist must be her mother.

'Mama, our visitors are arriving. Come and see.'

'Why should I need to see them arrive, dear? I have seen carriages before, and ladies walking.'

'But they are doing neither, Mama. Oh, do come, they are on bicycles.'

'Bicycles! Those infernal machines. How very unladylike.'

'Oh, no, Mama, I am quite sure Mrs Flint would never do anything inappropriate.'

'Do not contradict your mother, Euphemia,' but she did come over to the window and look at the spectacle. The two ladies drew up to the front of the manor and gracefully dismounted, handing the bicycles to the footmen. 'Will you take Miss Patricia for a stroll in the gardens, dear? You may take your tea after that.'

'Yes, Mama.'

Euphemia was glad of the excuse as she was desperate to interrogate her friend about the wonderful newfangled contraption.

Patricia's eyes sparkled. 'Oh, Phemie, it's ripping! You simply have to get one so we can go off on rides together.'

'I'd love to, but my mother disapproves.'

'Your mother would disapprove of Christmas if she could get away with it.'

'I know,' she sighed, 'and I so want one. I even sent off for a brochure. It arrived this morning, but it has vanished. I'll never have any freedom.'

'Buck up, it's just a setback. You can always send for another one. Or just get one from our supplier. I'm sure we still have the details. Come round after church and have a look. You can order one and have it delivered to us. Your mother need never know.'

'Oh, Pat! Would I dare? I'd get into such trouble.'

'What could she do? Lock you up? How much more restricted could your life get?'

'I don't know. I expect she'd find something.'

'But think of the thrill—it's like being a bird. Worth any punishment!'

'For a daughter of the cloth, you are a bad influence, Patricia Flint,' she smiled.

'But you're tempted, you know you are.'

'Of course I am. I've dreamed of nothing else since I first read that article in Girl's Own Paper.'

'Then get one. It's good for your health; it said so in the article.'

Euphemia gazed into the distance, imagining. Could she?

'Come and see it. They put them in the stables.'

The two girls glanced around to see if anyone was watching. Through the large parlour window they could see their mothers deep in conversation, not paying attention to the gardens. It was safe.

The bicycle was even more desirable in solid form. Euphemia stroked its polished handlebars.

'Have a go.'

'No, Pat, not here, that is going too far. What if I fall off and tear my frock?'

'I suppose you have a point there. I fell off once or twice before I got the knack. It would be better in a walking dress than your pretty tea gown. I shall invite you to our house when we go in for tea.'

'Speaking of which, we had better go in now or we shall be missed.'

The plan was somewhat thwarted, however, when Mrs Flint included Euphemia's mother in the invitation, which was eagerly taken up.

The following Sunday afternoon, the girls were asked to watch Pat's small siblings. Their mothers planned to look at the latest roses in the garden, saying they might also visit Mrs Wilkinson's garden for some advice about her chrysanthemums that had won prizes at the recent village fete.

'Why is my mother suddenly so keen on chrysanthemums? I suppose it must be the latest fad.'

'At least they are safely out of the house so I can show you the pamphlets.'

'Ooh, yes.'

The girls pored over pictures of bicycles and compared prices, while paying scant attention to the little ones, who seemed quite absorbed with their dolls. A selection was made and a letter written.

'I'll call at the Post Office first thing in the morning and send it off with a postal order.'

'I'll let you know when we receive a reply. It should be here in a few weeks. Ours were.'

Euphemia clapped her hands with excitement, but then her face fell. 'What will your parents think when another bicycle shows up here?'

'Oh, don't worry about that, I told them and they think it's a great joke. You know Father's not at all stuffy. He does believe in children obeying their parents, of course, but you haven't been specifically told not to, and it is in the best interest of your health, really.'

'I can hardly wait. And when the mothers get back, do you think we can slip out and have a go?'

'Of course. But whatever are the babies doing? Cecilia! Margaret! No! Dolly does not need a haircut, her hair does not grow like yours.' Pat managed to remove the scissors from her small sisters before any harm was done to Dolly's coiffure, and the girls spent the rest of the afternoon playing tea parties.

Their mothers took rather longer than expected and when they returned there was only time for some tea and cake before the visit drew to a close. It was looking likely that Euphemia's first ride would be on her own bicycle.

She found it hard to concentrate on anything else, even knitting the cycling sweater for which she had been thrilled to find a pattern in a magazine. She had to unravel one sleeve no less than five times before she got it right. She was sewing it up when she received the note from Pat that her bicycle had arrived.

Her fingers flew as she finished the last few stitches and hurriedly pulled it on over her everyday blouse. She fumbled with the hooks and eyes as she changed her day skirt for a tweed walking skirt, and almost forgot she was wearing her slippers. She dropped the button hook twice as she fastened her outdoor boots. Finally, she was ready, and hurried down the stairs. As she was in the hallway, being helped into her coat by a footman, her mother came out of the morning room, also dressed for walking.

'Oh, hello, Euphemia. Going somewhere?'

'Yes, Mama, Pat invited me over for tea.'

'How very nice. I am also visiting. Do not be late for supper. George, is the carriage ready?'

'Yes, my lady.'

But why was her mother using the carriage if dressed for walking? How very odd. Never mind, it would have been awkward if they had been going the same way and she had been caught.

She was slightly out of breath when she arrived at the vicarage. Maybe she should have asked to be dropped off in the carriage. But better not to arouse suspicions; she had always preferred to walk to the village if the weather was clement.

Pat greeted her. 'Oh, I'm so glad you weren't any earlier. Your mother was here.'

'My mother? How strange. I told her I was coming here and she said nothing about sharing a destination. But you say *was*?'

'Yes, she called for my mother and they went out. I think they took a hamper. She had the footman fetch something from round the back.'

'Maybe they are having a picnic. How mean not to invite us, but just as well, I suppose. So where is it? I simply cannot wait a moment longer.'

'Come on, it's this way.'

The bicycle was beautiful. Black and shiny and all hers.

Pat was wearing a walking dress of blue serge. 'Leave your coat behind. It's warm enough without it and they do flap about. Skirts are bad enough. I want to make some knickerbockers. I saw a pattern, but mother thinks it might be a step too far.'

'I should say so!'

'Oh, I do like your sweater.'

'Thank you, I only finished it today. I couldn't concentrate on anything not connected to the bicycle. It was only knitting this that kept me sane these last weeks. Even then, I kept making mistakes. It's just as well it was only for me. I couldn't in all conscience give away something I had unpicked so much. The wool is a bit thin in places.'

'Well, it looks fine, and very suitable.'

Not long after, Euphemia wished she had stuffed some padding into the leg of mutton sleeves of that sweater, when she fell off for the second time. 'Ouch!' She rubbed her elbow. 'Does it really get easier? This wasn't part of my dream of freedom.'

'Come on, you'll get the hang of it soon enough. Just keep pedalling; the faster you go the easier it is to balance.'

'That's easy for you to say.'

But she did catch on soon enough and the two girls had a lovely afternoon, pedalling along the lanes near the village. Euphemia laughed as she freewheeled down a long hill they had slogged up half an hour previously, Pat close behind her.

Suddenly she wobbled and her laugh turned to a scream as she neared the crossroads and saw two other ladies cycling towards them on a collision course, also freewheeling down a hill.

'Brake!' called Patricia, but Euphemia panicked and forgot how to stop. She wobbled and steered into the ditch, where she lay in a crumpled tangle of bicycle and hedge.

'Phemie!' The cry came, not just from Pat, but from one of the other ladies, who had managed to brake more or less decorously and had jumped from her machine and was running to the ditch.

Euphemia struggled to sit up, luckily unhurt, brushing mud and leaves from her sadly mangled cycling sweater, to stare into a most unexpected concerned face.

'Mother? What are you doing here?'

'The same as you, by the look of it,' laughed her mother. 'Are you hurt?'

'No, but I hope the bicycle is alright.'

'Infernal machine, you're more important.'

'But how come you're riding one if you hate them so much?'

'Did I say I hated them? I was intrigued that day when our friends here arrived on them. I had just that morning found your secretive little brochure, and it seemed they were everywhere. But Mrs Flint convinced me how useful they were, and I decided to try hers out.'

'But why not tell me? I was living in fear you would find out I had ordered one.'

'I thought you would laugh at me.'

'Mama, I would never do that.' But she could not keep the unladylike grin from sneaking onto her face, and the four ladies laughed themselves silly, before helping Euphemia from the ditch and riding slowly and carefully back to the vicarage for tea.

JOY

Ann Cooper

My greatest joy,
A cheeky grin,
A grubby hand slipped into mine,
Whisper of hair, soft on my cheek,
A sticky kiss,
"I love you, Nan."

HEAVEN AND HELL

Ann Cooper

A darkened room, stroking, touching,
Whispered words of love,
Trails of knowing kisses,
A burning fire, an explosion of stars.
You are in instant heaven.
I am condemned to hell,
For you love without loving,
While I love with my very soul.

THE CLOCK IS TICKING

Mike Hemstock

The clock is ticking,
Time passes quick.
Live for the moment,
Don't miss a tick.

The clock is ticking,
Everything's alive.
Searching for knowledge,
Reach for the skies.

The clock is ticking,
Time passes slow.
Which way to turn?
Which way to go?

The clock is ticking,
As we reach our prime.
We must be wary,
Not to run out of time.

The clock is ticking,
Time has passed by.
For some of the people,
It's their time to die.

DANDELIONS

Shirley McIntire

Being a creature of habit, Lady Winifred Peebody would get up when her hangover became intolerable, then, stumbling to the bathroom with barely-opened bloodshot eyes, she would slurp enough water to slake her dehydration-induced thirst, and wash down two paracetamols. Then Winnie would collapse again, praying that the painkillers, combined with a couple more hours' sleep would help her to feel more human.

Later, fully recovered, she would enjoy preparing for another night out at her local, formerly owned by her late, liver-pickled father, Sir Ewen Peebody. She would squash her bloated body into one of her numerous grubby ball gowns, then carefully arrange a trilby, rakishly, over the lank, greasy hair, which she would tease into a kiss-curl onto her forehead. The finale to this bizarre ensemble would be her make up: orange pan stick, doing its best to camouflage the clusters of blackheads, crimson lipstick forming a perfect 'cupid's bow', and a beauty spot blobbed on her left cheek. Head on one side she would examine the result in the crazed mirror. If her crêpy skin had a jaundiced tinge, Winnie would rummage in her sticky cosmetic bag, retrieve one of her gloopy lipsticks, and rub it generously on each cheek.

'Ah, now that's better,' she would smile, rubbing her tongue over her lipstick-smeared teeth. Satisfied, she would saunter to The Peebody Arms, resembling a passable caricature of a fairground Aunt Sally.

The regulars were used to Winnie—she was their only source of entertainment.

When she had put in her first intoxicated appearance, the well-to-do punters had huffed and puffed embarrassedly, but now the 'gentlemen' were secretly disappointed if Winnie decided to have a gin-soaked night in front of the telly. Very occasionally she would make drunken, aggressive resolutions to never set foot in the place again, but these would not last more than one night, and when she went in the following evening the excitement-starved customers would be almost forming an orderly queue to buy her pints of Strongbow.

After more cider she would be at her peak, continuing with her raucous singing, whilst lurching from one punter to another, touching them suggestively as she went. Most of the customers, whilst encouraging this familiar finale, knew better than to respond in any other way than hearty laughter.

There had been a newcomer once, who'd had the temerity to reciprocate the groping, but this had been the trigger for Winnie's underlying aggression to come to the fore, and she had been terrifying in her volley of expletives.

'What the hell do you think you're doing? There I am just having a sing-song and a pint, and you start touching me up, you perv,' she'd snarled, 'I've a good mind to call the police. I could have you done for sexual assault.'

The red-faced hapless target had looked around with incredulity. 'You saw her,' he'd begged the regulars. 'You saw what she did to me, and to some of you lot, too. Christ, she was asking for it, wasn't she?'

The Harris Tweed Brigade had looked down and shuffled their feet uncomfortably; there had been a lot of throat clearing and retreats to the Gents.

They had feared, correctly, that Winnie had been just getting into her stride and had been preparing herself for "Lady Peebody mode".

Suddenly her voice had trilled, 'Do you know who I am? Do you know just whom you've offended? I am Lady Peebody of Peebody Hall and you've had the audacity to touch my tits…ahem, I mean bosoms. What have you got to say for yourself?'

'But you …' His voice had petered out miserably as he had seen the blank looks on the faces of the other customers and bar staff. At that point he'd sunk the remains of his pint and slunk out of the pub.

Eventually time had been called and, as usual, Winnie had refused to leave and had had to be summarily ejected from the Peebody Arms. Her nights out often ended like that, but there were never any hard feelings. She was always welcomed back as usual the following evening.

How she managed to get home each night was as much a mystery to her as it was to everyone else; except that is for that memorable occasion when she fell flat on her face in Caterpillar Meadow after slipping in a steamy cowpat. What a fall!

Winnie had no idea how much time had elapsed before she awoke to the sound of heavily-gushing water. Slowly lifting her head, she saw a gigantic carthorse emptying his bladder right next to her, and as the considerable jet ricocheted off the grass, her face and head caught most of the spray.

'What the hell…?' she slurred thickly.

His toilet complete, Dobbin ambled off, tearing up grass, oblivious to his sodden victim who was now very much awake. Winnie, however had nothing but gratitude for the horse's timely spraying—Lady Peabody would have been terribly embarrassed if one of the villagers had discovered her—trilby askew and face caked in mud, or worse!

‘Thank you, God,’ she whispered easing onto her knees. Then, balancing precariously on her haunches, she looked around in a state of drunken euphoria; amazingly it was nearly light. How long had she been there? No matter, the sun was rising and it felt good to be alive. This feeling was all too familiar, and she knew it must be appreciated before it was replaced by an inevitable thunderous hangover.

However, for the time being, life was great, and she knew that she must find a memento of that moment of ecstasy. *What can I take*? she wondered, desperate for the occasion to be etched in her memory. Scratching with concentration at her horse-uriney hair, she glanced in surprise at the damp, orange spikes clinging to her grubby nails and fingertips. Their colour was beautiful, but what were they? Then she saw them—a patch of dandelions, languishing adjacent to the offending cowpat. To her inebriated eyes they were the most wonderful flowers ever, and she tried to remember a poem from school. *Now what was it*? she mused.

‘Ah hah,’ she shouted, ‘by George I’ve got it, “A Host of Golden Dandelions”, something about fluttering and dancing in the wind, written by William somebody or other. She scratched her head again, trying to remember. ‘Oh, well, something like that,’ she sighed.

It mattered not that this particular host was squashed almost flat by her fall. Winnie just knew she had to have them, and set about dragging a straggly, soily handful from the reluctant sod. Clutching her weeds like a bridal bouquet, she staggered home, humming and giggling to “Here Comes the Bride”.

Towards the end of her zig-zaggy journey she focused all her concentration on them and, by the time she reached Peebody Hall, the dandelions had become her most prized possession.

She shuffled on her ample backside down to the basement kitchen.

'Now then, where shall we put you, my lovelies?' she asked the flowers, smiling at them beatifically. The greasy, neglected room was bereft of any kind of vase and, after a short time of rummaging around in vain, truth be told, Winnie was becoming cheesed off.

'Oh, I don't believe this!' she said savagely and, in desperation, barely able to keep her aching eyes open, she grabbed a bottle of semi skimmed, emptied its contents, filled it with water and plonked the dandelions unceremoniously into their makeshift vase. Actually, sick and tired of them by now—their charm was wearing thin—nevertheless, she made her way back up the stairs, then up another flight to her bedroom, slopping milky water in her wake.

Lurching towards the windowsill, she slammed the irritating bottle of weeds down, and then launched herself onto her bed.

'Satisfied are you?' she snarled at them.

In three seconds flat she was snoring and dribbling like an adenoidal baby.

The next thing she knew, watery sunshine was winking at her through the threadbare curtains, exacerbating a dull ache at the back of her eyeballs. But that wasn't all. Winnie was absolutely wet through. All her clothes (she always slept fully clothed), her sheets, and even part of her pillow were sodden. More puzzled than perturbed, she eased her soggy way out of bed and squinted at the clock. She had slept a full ten hours.

Apart from the customary headache, she felt marvellous, and had never had such a good night's sleep in all her adult life. *Oh, if only it could be like this every night*, she thought wistfully, and turned over for another couple of hour's kip, unconcerned by her smelly, wet bed.

By evening her headache had lifted enough to go to the pub, as usual, and Winnie was cheered by her welcome from the bored village menfolk. For their part, they were relieved the entertainment had arrived, and happily dug into their pockets to make sure Winnie began performing as quickly as possible. They weren't disappointed. In less than an hour she had downed four pints of her favourite tipple and the floorshow had begun. This consisted of telling the filthiest jokes imaginable and lustily singing ribald rugby songs. She dredged her sluggish mind back to her Finishing School days when she had been the mascot and bike of the local Rugby club. She'd had a wonderful year or so before her inevitable expulsion, and had never forgotten those stolen nights. Winnie was always delighted that more and more crude jokes and songs returned to her befuddled memory when she was drunk. Her pièce de résistance was the most vulgar version of "The German Officers Crossed the Line, parlez-vous", imaginable.

The next day was Edna Daft's cleaning session at Peebody Hall. Winnie couldn't bear the roar of the vacuum cleaner when she was hungover, so Edna did her stint in the evening. Quickly, she sloshed a greasy dishcloth round the kitchen and blew the top layer of dust from the old fashioned ornaments in the morning room. Then it was the lounge with its dusty red velvet curtains and cobwebby chandeliers, and Edna gave that a perfunctory once over.

Finally she knew it could not be put off any longer. She had to tackle Winnie's bedroom, a disgusting place where the smell of sweat, booze and stomach gases mingled nauseatingly.

She rummaged deep into the kangaroo pocket of her tabard and brought out her trusty jar of Vick. Plunging her middle finger into the sticky vapour, she managed to force a generous dollop up each nostril. She'd learned this clever trick from watching Quincy on daytime TV. She idolised the US Coroner and had all his episodes on video. Edna remembered with gratitude the sight of her hero putting Vick up his nose when dealing with a particularly smelly corpse.

Breathing in the vapours until her eyes watered, she flung open the bedroom door, horrified to find that even the magical properties of Vick could not mask the stink of stale urine, jostling with the usual noxious, nauseating smells.

'Well, if this isn't the limit,' she sneered. 'The dirty cow must have peed herself!'

In just seven minutes Edna Daft had flicked a duster over the furniture, skimmed the carpet with the battered hoover, then, rubbish bin in one hand and a bottle of dead weeds in the other, she backed out of the room, trying not to breathe.

Sometime later, Winnie reeled into the same room and gratefully sank into bed, only to wake up after an hour for the toilet. She was, initially, disappointed, but still too drunk to think much about it. However, at the fourth bladder-emptying session, peeing gushingly, she thought the sound seemed familiar. *Now what could it be? What does that remind me of*? she thought woozily.

Then she remembered her damp encounter with Dobbin in Caterpillar Meadow, and how his noisy weeing had saved her from embarrassment. This train of muddled thoughts led to the recollection of the flowers she had picked at the same time, which she'd not glanced at since.

Wearily trudging back to bed, Winnie looked at the windowsill where her bouquet had resided. There was nothing there, not even the empty bottle. She neither knew nor cared what had happened to them; all she wanted was a bit more sleep. After all, there were tons of them in Caterpillar Meadow; she could always pick more if the mood took her.

Time passed and, to her disappointment, her toilet-interrupted nights were back as bad as ever. It seemed the halcyon period of peaceful sleep had never happened; she was worn out.

One day, after an especially heavy night in the Watering Hole, she did not surface completely until five pm, so decided virtuously not to go to the pub that night, and would have a couple of gins in front of the telly. While she was in this healthy frame of mind, she thought she'd take a stroll, and finished up in Caterpillar Meadow, where she spotted the dandelions.

This time she picked a huge bunch and found a proper vase, more befitting their beauty than a milk bottle, then placed them once again on her bedroom windowsill. That night she slept without any toilet interruptions. Still, she'd only had some gin and she was desperately missing her cider.

The next evening she was back to her usual consumption but, again, she slept solidly, although her bed was sodden when she did wake up. It was like déjà vu and Winnie could not believe her luck.

This continued throughout the next few nights—coincidentally until the latest bunch of dandelions wilted. Then the lavatorial visits began again in earnest.

Lady Winifred Peabody set herself the task of getting to the root of the problem and, by the process of elimination, she concluded that the dandelions were her saviour.

She tested this theory many times over several drunken nights, and it was foolproof. On the nights she had no dandelions she awoke several times for the toilet, but when they were on the shelf she didn't, and her bed was satisfactorily soaked the following morning.

Winnie's life turned around, although she was still hung over every day, but at least she knew she could rely on sleeping soundly after her drinking binges.

Then she became greedy. Secure in the knowledge that her slumbers would not be interrupted, she increased her alcohol intake. Very soon, with the assistance of her audience at The Peebody Arms, she was up to twenty pints a night, and still the dandelions worked their charm. Unfortunately the rest is history:-

Miss Peebody has passed away;
they think she may have drowned.
Her deathbed was a soggy mess
when she was finally found.
Her petard was well hoisted;
I think you will agree,
those dandelions had caused her fate;
she'd drowned in her own wee.
Let's not forget the benefits
she gave in her demise.
Where would we be without Miss Pee
and her true sacrifice?
If she'd not stumbled headlong,
that night so long ago,

the dandelions' secret,
no one would ever know.
The world would be so different,
a sadder, dryer place.
We must not underestimate
this improved human race.
We can drink and have a skinful
without that nagging dread
of waking up six times each night
and leaving our warm bed.
The dandelions work their charm
as everybody knows,
they bring on Enuresis;
you just lay there, and it flows.
Damp beds each day are nothing
when you've had a full night's snooze,
so it's thanks to Lady Peebody
that we can sup more booze.

LIFE'S JOURNEY

Alfred J Holt

We speed from the darkened tunnel,
The tracks shining bright in the light;
It shoots over chasms and hills,
And sinks low into the night.

We pause at the sorrow stations,
We race past the valley of tears,
Where our hearts were full and brave,
Now filled with repining and fears.

But the road of this perilous journey
The hand of the master has made;
With all its vexation and dangers,
We are always sad and afraid.

The burning-red pit ever waiting
For all those who tread the wrong path,
Running, shouting, and mayhem,
We face the horns in the hearth.

The life that we lead is now futile,
Disappearing into a black haze,
Back into the same darkened tunnel.
It's time to depart from life's maze.

JACK PIZER

David Brailsford

You may think I'm stupid, but I tell you this...I know who it is.

It's John Pizer, known in the street rumours as Leather Apron.

About thirty years old and a shoemaker.

It's said, 'A working class man will be most suspect, 'cos your toffs don't turn to serial killing, and that's a fact.'

Jack's a boot finisher, living in the heart of Whitechapel, well known among the prozzies, or bangtails, as we call 'em.

They fear 'im, 'cos he hates 'em with a devilish rage and is extremely dangerous, carrying a razor-sharp knife, threatening to cut their throats.

Many bangtails have complained to the police about his threats, and are prepared to testify, which is unusual for them. They allege that, for several years, he kicked, bruised and injured them.

Only a few weeks before the first prozzie was murdered, he had drawn a knife on a street girl called Widow Annie and declared, grinning like a devil, he was going to 'rip 'er up'.

These words would haunt 'im, for during the police investigation, they were the very words received in an anonymous letter from someone claiming to be the killer.

Not only that, pieces of bloodstained leather apron, exactly like that in his boot-finishing workshop, were found next to the bodies of Annie Chapman and Catherine Eddowes.

After he was arrested for questioning, on the tenth of September, a large number of sharp knives were removed from his shop.

Soon after, his house was surrounded by an angry mob and, if the police hadn't broken it up, Jack would have lost his life...for sure.

A bangtail named Violina witnessed an argument between a man and one of her friends on Hanbury Street. This man pulled out a knife, threatening to 'rip 'er up'.

At an identification parade Violina picked out Jack, but the prozzie he threatened never came forward, so the case didn't reach court.

Maybe, she was the one found dead that night.

Violina couldn't remember what night the incident had occurred, but thought it was around the time of the Hanbury Street murder.

What more proof do we need?

He was the Ripper all right... No doubt about it.

THE RED PLANET

Barrie J Kinsella

I'm set in the stars,
They have named me Mars,
Nestling between two moons,
The Romans revered me
As their god of war.
My mountains higher, canyons deeper
Than other planets in my surround,
The solar systems largest volcano;
My rivers flowed, streams meandered,
The lakes held impenetrable mysteries.
Millenniums have passed, no water today
Gives life to my planet, only frozen remains
Of ice caps above underground streams.
Come visit me when you are able.
I have waited here for aeons,
Always to remain while the galaxy reigns,
Prompting curiosity which cannot be satisfied.
Some things you can never understand,
Each time you tilt your head
To look at me and see
The red planet watching thee.

THE MONDAY CLUB. THE MISUNDERSTANDING

Dawn Raffle

Joe Bradshaw changed his lifestyle after Sheila, his wife, died. She'd had rigid views about what she saw as the demon drink, compromising only at Christmas, or a do at the golf club, when a small glass of sherry was permitted. His brother in law, Charles, a Presbyterian minister, shared the same narrow view, on his obligatory visit, casting baleful eyes on the half-empty whisky bottle on Joe's coffee table, and suggesting that Joe took up a hobby more respectful to Sheila's memory. It sparked off a rebellion that had been building within Joe for forty-five years. The subservient worm had turned. No more keeping quiet and putting up with things. He threw Charles out of the house.

Everyone in the family, that is Shelia's family, was shocked. It was said grief had unhinged his mind. Within months he had sold up, and moved to a small village on the borders of Derbyshire, near to his only relative, his sister, Vera, and found that life began at seventy. Especially at the local pub called the Corner Pin, where he regularly called in on a Monday afternoon and met up with new-found friends, George, Mo, Ralph, Jack, Bill and Frank. The funny incidents and the stories told gave Joe a new hobby—writing—and he recorded some of the events shared.

One Monday afternoon Joe was sitting in the Corner Pin when George came in.

"I'd cover your scooter up, it looks like rain," they all shouted.

George looked round at his mates and then nodded towards Lisa, the barmaid. "Lisa always wipes it down for me, part of the job."

"With blades fixed to the wheels you could cut the nettles on the footpath on your way down," said Mo.

"Nettles are easy, it's dog crap on wheels that's problem," George answered.

Ralph came up to the bar, joining in the banter. "You're right. Do you know? A walk down the footpath to the Corner Pin is better than any dance class. True, think about it. To keep shoes clean, take a step to the side, one forward, one back, and sway, to avoid stepped-in bits, and a quick twirl round the larger offerings of horse muck, and you're dancing the tango. I reckon a walk the other way to the village and you'd do a fair quickstep. What do you think, Jack?"

Jack eased himself back into his seat and said, "Me and my missus used to go dancing."

"What, down footpath?" Lisa chipped in as she pulled Ralph a pint.

Jack passed his glass over to be filled. "No, seriously, we went every week for a year. We were good an' all, but we packed it in."

"Why?" asked Frank, lifting his head out of his paper.

Jack sighed. "Well…it was the Blackpool trip that done it." He paused while he sorted his change.

"And?" Lisa prompted.

Jack shook his head. "Wife couldn't wait to get to the tower ballroom, and there we were, strutting like peacocks, waltz, rumba, quickstep, the lot. Then friends asked us why we were dancing in the corner. That's when we realised…" He gave a shrug. "It was the dance class, too many learners, no space, you see. All that tuition, and all we could do was dance in the corner."

"That's why he comes in the Corner Pin; he's comfortable in the corner," Mo said.

Laughter filled the bar. Joe enjoyed it.

"Anyone want a pint before I go out for a fag?" Lisa asked. "Bill, you okay?" He nodded, and continued to scan the racing pages in his paper.

Mo held up his empty glass. "I'll have one."

"Mo, you've got one in," Lisa said. "Anyone else? Joe, you alright?"

Joe grinned and said, "I'll last till you get back,"

George said, "I'll have another tot."

Standing outside, Lisa could hear them laughing. She loved Monday afternoons when they all came to the pub. They discussed and laughed about everything, jokes a speciality. Problems sorted, solutions found. Many a stranger, calling in for a quick pint, stayed and enjoyed the banter. Joe had fitted in well, a bit quiet but getting more involved with the teasing and jokes.

Walking back inside, she was met with, "Thought you were on holiday."

She smiled sweetly, as she picked up Ralph's glass on her way to the bar. "If I'd any sense I'd have a holiday on Mondays."

"Oh, you'd miss us," Mo retorted. They all laughed, except Bill, who got up and went through to the toilets.

They all looked at each other. Ralph pulled a face. "What's up with him? He's not said much today."

George frowned. "I don't know. He's been like it since he came in. Lisa, has he said anything to you?"

"I think he's fell out with Daisy. I didn't get the gist of it, and I was busy serving as he was talking. I'll have a few words when he comes back in."

George said, "Well, he's hardly spoken so far. Maybe he doesn't want us to know."

"Shush…." Ralph said, as Bill walked back in and sat down.

Lisa came round from the back of the bar, and sat on a stool. "Come on, Bill, cheer up."

All eyes were on him. He looked at Lisa, and said, "As I told you, I upset Daisy. I'd a bit too much to drink and I broke it off." He shrugged his shoulders. "Now I have to face her mother."

Everyone was silent. Daisy and Bill had been together a long time.

"Better you than me," George said. "I wouldn't like to be the wrong side of Daisy's mother."

Frank gave a low whistle. "Don't envy you, mate, she's a vicious devil when she's upset. Didn't she knock her husband clean out the front door when she found out about his bit on the side?"

"That was a long while ago. She's calmed down a bit since she's got older," countered Mo.

"Do you like hospital food?" Ralph said, stifling a laugh.

Bill glanced round at his mates. "You're a fat lot of help."

Jack offered everyone a pinch of snuff.

Ralph grimaced. "No, thanks, last pinch was more like coal dust." The nods of the others said the same thing.

Lisa stood up, and walked back to the bar saying, "Get Daisy a present, something nice, a piece offering."

Bill shook his head. "I don't know… Anyway, I'm skint."

Several options were put forward. Ralph suggested a plant, and asked Mo if he had any on his allotment.

Mo answered, "Trouble is they're not ready yet, perhaps in a week or two. But you can buy plants in a bottle, they're alright. Anyhow, you've been together years. She'll come round. It can be fixed."

Bill said, "No, it can't! I've been everywhere, even the antique shop."

Lisa looked puzzled; in fact, they all did. "What's the antique shop got to do with it?" she queried.

Bill answered, "The spout had a piece missing."

"Just a minute," Lisa said, "what are we talking about?"

Bill looked at her as if she was stupid. "I already told you: The antique tea pot. The one that belonged to Daisy's grandmother, I knocked it off the shelf when I was drunk. The spout broke off."

Lisa scrunched forward, her shoulders shaking with laughter. When she calmed down she said, "Oh, my God, Bill, I'm sorry. What, with everyone talking at the bar I didn't catch all you said. I thought…you'd got problems with Daisy."

Joe leaned forward, and with his new found bravado said, "So you and Daisy aren't splitting up?"

The laughter that followed didn't amuse Bill. He snapped, "You may think it's funny, but it's a family heirloom, and I'm in deep trouble. It's nothing to laugh at."

George managed to splutter, "We don't think it's funny, and we are concerned."

Bill looked round at them all laughing. "You all look concerned." But his mouth twitched, and he smiled, then laughed and, between guffaws, managed to gasp, "When her mother finds out, I'm dead. I can't fix it."

Lisa held up a bottle of whisky. "Try this bottle," she said.

Bill pointed his finger at her. "That won't work."

She gave a wry smile. “It will, if you drink it before you tell Daisy’s mother.”

The laughter started again, and soon the pub rang with the sound. Lisa served another round of drinks as the hilarity and banter continued. When she went out for another cigarette, she winked at Joe.

He felt included. *‘Another issue sorted by the Monday club, and I was part of it,’* he thought.

SOUND OF THE SEA

Ann Cooper

Heavy grey skies, threatening rain,
Empty fairground, deserted beaches,
The only sound, the restless sea.
Slap and suck, slap and suck.

Depressed, lonely, I trudge along;
No-one to care, family, friends, all gone;
Drink from my bottle to forget.
Slap and suck, slap and suck.

I stagger, rolling like the sea,
Sit on the harbour wall to rest,
Hand shaking, light my last cigarette.
Slap and suck, slap and suck.

Take another swig from my bottle;
There's a buzzing in my brain;
I'm hearing voices, calling me.
Slap and suck, slap and suck.

Come to me, come to me,
Leave your world, let it be;
Explore the treasures of the sea.
Slap and suck, slap and suck.

Am I going mad? Drain my bottle.
The voices ring louder in my head,
Echoing round and round in my brain.
Slap and suck, slap and suck.

Come, take that final leap,
Come and slip into the deep,
Find comfort in eternal sleep.
Slap and suck, slap and suck.

Heavy grey skies, threatening rain,
Empty fairground, deserted beaches,
Bottle floating on the restless sea.
Slap and suck, slap and suck.

AMBROSIA

Mike Hemstock

The food and drink of the gods
Is there for all to share.
For everlasting youth and beauty,
Be anointed with it.

We are as young as we feel.
Keep taking the elixir of life.
Even the old are rejuvenated.
Live life to the full.

It's something sweet and pleasant.
Everyone needs a slice.
Take a finely-flavoured beverage.
Enjoy the ambrosia of life.

FALLEN FRUITS

Mike Hemstock

Fallen fruits lie on the earth,
Harvest has been gathered.
In the fertile, breeding grounds
There is grain for all to share.
The warm breeze of autumn
Changes to cooler days;
Dew forms on the spiders' webs;
Flimsy threads, floating in the breeze
Can be seen in the frosty air.

The signs of winter appear!

RETRIBUTION

Angela Rigley

Terry had no cause to complain about his life. And now he had the extra excitement of being accepted as a contestant on the popular quiz show 'Generalities', and had been invited by the TV studios to go for a preliminary round. He had no concerns on that score. He would sail through it, his exceptional knowledge standing him in good stead. Everybody said he would walk it. He wasn't a vain man, but recognition for his exceptional abilities wouldn't go amiss.

He loved his job as the head of the computer programming section at Lansdowns. What's more, he knew himself to be extremely adept at it. Having attended the local grammar school, and received a first class honours degree at Cambridge, he had beaten hundreds of other candidates for the job, and single-handedly, in his opinion, built up the firm to be the most prestigious business in the area.

His pretty wife, Claire, a successful barrister, had also grown up in the town. Their older son, Jason, the most popular boy in the school, outperformed all his fellow pupils at sport. He played basketball for the county and they had come top of the league, while Jonathon, his younger son, more of an academic, preferred books to sports, and planned on becoming an accountant.

He couldn't be regarded as boastful, just counted the blessings life bestowed upon him, and knew his colleagues envied his grand five–bedroomed house, the many rooms kept scrupulous by the cleaning lady whom they employed three days a week.

And the garden! Well, no other garden in the area could compare to it. The colourful flowerbeds, ornate rockeries and large ornamental statues were a treat to behold.

Not that he took all the credit for it, of course. His gardener, Fred, did most of the work, but Terry still had to see that the petunias and pansies were planted in the sunniest positions, and the shrubs and hedges were clipped to exactly the right shape.

Arriving at the studios in plenty of time, he entered with his head high. *Confidence and self-assurance: that's half the game with an opponent,* he told himself.

A short, balding man, wearing modern, rimless spectacles, looked up from his newspaper, and seemed about to speak, but the floor manager came in, saying, "I'm John. Please follow me, and we'll make a start."

They made their way into a small room off the main studio, and John asked them a few general knowledge questions, insultingly easy ones. Terry left feeling even more positive than when he'd arrived.

Later that evening, after Claire had washed the dishes, and the boys had gone to their rooms to do their homework, Terry lolled on the settee in front of the television.

"What was the name of the other contestant you were telling me about earlier?" Claire asked as she sat opposite him.

"Joseph Bright or…no, I think it was Bridges."

"That rings a bell. Wasn't there a boy at school with that name? A puny little boy with round National Health glasses, and braces, always being picked on and bullied by the bigger boys?"

"I don't remember. I didn't mix with the other boys much, they weren't my type. Anyway, I don't want to be reminded of those days." He changed channels on the television and became absorbed in a nature programme, leaving Claire to her Sudoku puzzle.

Much later that night, Terry tossed and turned, unable

to sleep. Claire's apparently innocent observation had struck a raw cord in his memory. It hadn't been his fault though, had it? He wouldn't have thrown the football boot onto the roof, or dunked the boy's head in the horse trough down the lane if the other boys hadn't egged him on, would he?

The following morning he awoke feeling wretched, the dark circles beneath his eyes proof of his disturbed sleep. Even a strong, black coffee failed to revive him. The knowing look on Claire's face did not help. She had taken the day off work to go with him for moral support, so he asked her to drive. She seemed slightly taken aback, because he usually insisted on driving everywhere himself, but she took the car keys from him without speaking.

Once in the waiting room, Terry paced up and down, trying to calm himself by silently counting to one hundred. His opponent entered and walked straight up to Claire, who had been examining a picture of a celebrity whose name he knew he should know, but could not remember.

"Well, hello," drawled Joseph in a strange accent. "It's Claire, isn't it? How lovely to see you after all this time.

I've been working in America and have just moved back to the area. You haven't changed a bit, still as beautiful as ever." He lowered his voice, nodding in Terry's direction. "You married him, then? I thought I recognized him yesterday, but wasn't sure. I remember you two being an item at school."

Terry could barely hear him, but he made out the words, "I was always jealous." Beginning to seethe inwardly, he wondered whether to intervene. How dare they talk about him as if he were not there? As he was about to march over to the man and give him a piece of his mind, John came in and ushered them into the studio.

Claire found a seat in the front of the audience section, and the two protagonists were shown to their podiums. Terry's self-confidence returned once the questions started, and he pulled out a sizeable lead.

Then the quizmaster asked, "What was the name of the song, sung in 1965, by Sam and the Pharaohs? Woolly..." Terry knew the answer: 'bully', but the image of his dreams the night before reared up in his head, and he hesitated a fraction of a second too long. Joseph pressed before him. After that it went downhill. His opponent beat him to the buzzer every time and the show ended with a resounding victory for the other man.

He had never been so humiliated in all his life. In the vain hope of avoiding a confrontation with his former classmate, he pulled Claire quickly through the foyer, hoping to leave before anybody else.

Foiling his attempt, however, a voice called from behind, "Better luck next time, old chap. By the way, I heard from your introduction that you work at Lansdowns?"

Terry turned, wondering what could be coming next.

"So don't be late for work on Monday because, in case you haven't heard...I start work there next week as the general manager."

A SONNET

Alfred J Holt

I think, sometimes, my heart is like a bee
That hovers through the summer months, and sings,
Gathering nectar, from all flowering things
In garden plots or on the meadow lea.

About my busyness from morn till late,
Then onward to my hive, with heavy wings;
Full with sweetness, in the confinement brings,
Heedlessness of my approaching fate.

But with my full heart I will come to thee,
And empty out what's captured there inside.
Bared and innocent, nothing can I hide,
Just love and joyfulness, for you to see.

The honey-gathered gold of my sweet love,
These gifts flow free from heaven above.

CAT DOOR

by Tiggie, a tabby cat,
translated by Dianne Rasmussen (aka MD)

Well, the new year seems to be rushing along. For Christmas we had a new cat door fitted that was programmed so only the four of us could get in. It seemed to work at first, but then our neighbour, Walter, who had been used to coming into our house whenever he liked, rushed at it with such force he broke the plastic locking device. Mind you, I think something must have been wrong with it to start with. Our carer—MD—has managed to get a new one sent and, when she gets it 'programmed', we should all be happy, so she says. I think happiness is about more than 'a working cat door'.

I'm not sure where I stand with Walter, the ginger cat next door, who used to be such a good friend. Since the day when I followed Boswell and the others into the house, as a show of loyalty to our 'family', leaving Walter standing alone, he seems to be rather cool towards me. I suppose I should expect that, but I can't help feeling rather sad.

When I went into the garden last week, he was talking to a pretty, little tabby and white cat called Penny. Her house backs onto our garden and she often comes over. She just wants to play. Bozzie says she's very friendly, and he rather likes her. MD plays with her sometimes and is obviously fond of her. I tried to chase her off once but she just lay on her back and said, "You can attack me if you like, but I only want to be friends." MD came over and bent down to stroke her asking, "Can't you two be mates?"

What is this business of being friends? MD says that as domesticated cats we do not have to worry about our 'basic instincts'. She feeds us, provides a home and has made sure we cannot reproduce. So what is there left for us to do? We can protect our territory, but this sometimes leads to fighting with other cats who want the same piece of land. We can play. Play is, I suppose, pretending to hunt for food by chasing woolly toys and cat nip mice. Of course, some cats chase real mice and catch birds, but only for fun, not for food.

MD says she wishes we only pretended to fight for territory. "If only you could try to get on with each other," she says. "You could be in the garden at different times, and not interfere with what the others want to do, and if you met you could just meow a greeting. Life would be much more peaceful."

She sighs as Jinny and Frances come banging through the cat door as if pursued by ten thousand demons.

The trouble is that, even in the house, the four of us don't always act like friends. We have lots of energy and sometimes we look for interesting ways to use it. Chasing a catnip mouse, pulled around on a long piece of string can be good fun, but MD usually gets tired before we do. Then we toss the mouse around by ourselves, but we argue about who gets to chase it, and that sometimes leads to little scraps. We don't draw blood but Jinny screams as if she is being torn apart. When MD comes to see what's happening, she runs under a chair, but as soon as MD is sure everyone is alright, she comes out and starts to fight again.

As I said, we don't intend to hurt each other but accidents happen. If we who are family are not always friendly, then it's not likely we can remain friendly with all the 'outside' cats, now is it?

Penny says, "I'm friendly with everyone. I get on well with Walter, and I talk to Brownie at a distance. I even greet Whitey on occasions when he is not busy chasing his dinner." The other cats don't try to attack Penny and she says that proves her way is best. The thing is, she does all this in our garden, not her own. Hers is very small, has very little grass, but lots of concrete, and tubs planted with flowers, so she doesn't stay there much. No-one wants to add that to their territory.

Walter's is big, but his people grow vegetables and they do as much as they can to stop cats digging in it. I don't know what sort Whitey and Brownie have, but Walter says it doesn't matter because boys like to explore other places and see if they can find anything interesting. I suppose we all want what we consider to be 'the best', but we don't always agree about what is worth having.

All of this doesn't solve the problem of how to keep the other cats out of our house once they're in the garden. MD says she can't afford to feed everyone who drops in, so she will just have to get the cat door sorted.

A CHRISTMAS RE-UNION

Tony Butler

On Christmas Eve he sat waiting on a bench in the park, waiting for me to invite him in. He hadn't moved since he'd pushed the envelope through the door of my flat the morning before. Hunched over against the biting cold, Simon waited.

He was one of my exes whom I had dumped two years before on Boxing Day, after he'd used all his savings to buy me the gorgeous, but extortionately-expensive Cartier watch I had wanted. But Simon was so boring, especially in bed, and he got on my nerves, following me around like a puppy.

I opened his letter.

'My darling Sue, I miss you so much. I can't eat or sleep properly without you. I keep remembering your touch and the way you smiled at me. I will do anything to be with you again. I have just won two-million pounds on the lottery, which is why I am writing to you. Take me back and I will sign the account over to you. Please, please, I'm begging you. Take me back!'

A millionaire, my arse! I thought at first, but opened the enclosed bank statement, proving he was.

I left the flat and hurried into the park, over to where Simon still sat.

You can sleep with me until you've signed the document tomorrow, but, then you're gone, I thought, smiling at him.

Simon did not return my smile, just stared at me with dead, unseeing eyes.

'Merry Christmas, Darling,' mocked the card, held in his frozen grip

A SNOWY BIRTHDAY

Angela Rigley

"Mum, Mum," Jeanie called as she looked out the window on her tenth birthday and saw the garden covered in sparkling white snow.

Her mother came rushing into the bedroom. "What's the matter, darling?"

"Just look outside."

"Oh, the snow, yes, I've seen it." Mum looked a bit gloomy.

"But isn't it just fab! I can go out and build a snowman after we've been to the hospital."

Dad came in and, when he wished her, "Happy birthday, sweetheart," he didn't seem very cheerful either.

Then it dawned on her. "We will still be able to go to the hospital, won't we?"

"Well, that's just it; we might not be able to dig the car out."

"But, Dad, we must! I've been waiting all my life for the doctors to take off my leg braces, and today's the day."

"I know, sweetheart, I know what it means to you. We'll do our very best to get you there. Tell you what, I'll go and ring Uncle John to see what the main roads are like."

Jeanie had been full of excitement when she had first woken up. Today was going to have been the best day of her life, but now she couldn't take her eyes off the white scene outside.

They just had to get to the hospital, they had to. She would even wheel herself in her wheelchair if necessary.

Mum gave Jeanie a cuddle. “Get dressed, darling. You can wear your favourite purple jumper. Then you can open your presents.”

She had asked for a mobile phone for her birthday, and Mum had said she was too young, but she hoped she had won her dad round. She could usually persuade him to her way of thinking, much to Mum’s annoyance.

The luminous pink present looked most likely to be a mobile phone, but eagerly ripping off the paper, disappointment filled her when she took out a box containing a bottle of fancy bubble bath.

“Thanks, Mum.” Trying hard to put on a brave face, she opened the other presents, but she could tell by their shape that none of them would be a phone.

Eating her breakfast, she remembered it would soon be Christmas, so she could ask Santa for a phone. She knew he didn’t really exist, it was actually Dad, but she liked to keep up the pretence, by saying, “But Santa can bring me that,” if Mum told her she couldn’t afford something.

But the disappointment about the mobile was nothing compared with not being able to dig out the car, and go to the hospital. Today she was supposed to be walking on her own, and the wheelchair would have been put away, once the strength in her legs had built up, and it looked like the snow that had looked so pretty earlier was going to dash her dreams.

“Come on, darling, I’m sure Dad will be able to sort something out.” Mum didn’t sound too convincing, but Jeanie clung onto the hope, as she heard her dad talking on the phone in the front room.

Then he rushed into the kitchen, his face shining. “Yes, Uncle John says the main roads are almost clear, so I’ll go and shovel the snow off the drive while you finish your breakfast, then we’ll be on our way.

I know your appointment isn't until eleven o'clock but we'll go early in case there are any hold-ups."

Jeanie clapped her hands in glee and reached up and kissed him. "Thank you, Dad." Itching to go out and help him clear the snow, she knew in her heart that she would only have been in his way, so watched through the side window until, after what seemed like an eternity, the drive had been cleared.

Although the snow still covered their street, Jeanie had confidence in her dad and, despite her mum's gasps every time they skidded, they eventually made it safely to the main road, and arrived at the hospital in time.

The doctors checked the x-rays and were well pleased with Jeanie. She held her breath as the braces were removed for the last time and she stood unaided. Biting her lip, she took some tentative steps and almost fell, but her dad grabbed her in time. Her legs felt very weak but the exercises she had been doing to strengthen them must have helped because persevering, slowly taking one step at a time, she managed to walk across the room and back. Everyone clapped. She beamed, never having felt so special.

Afterwards, as they sat drinking tea in the café, Mum delved into her handbag and took out a parcel. "One more present, darling, for being such a brave girl."

Jeanie tore off the paper and screamed with delight. A pink mobile phone with an inbuilt camera, just like the one she had seen in the catalogue.

"This really is the best day of my life," she cried. "Now I can walk on my own I'll be able to build a snowman, and take a photo of it on my mobile to show to all my friends on Facebook."

WE ALL NEED PEOPLE

Ann Cooper

Susie should have been happy and contented, for she lived with loving parents and her two teasing, but protective, brothers. Their home was a comfortable roost in a sheltered spot under the pier. Susie could hover and dive and soar through the skies. Fish were plentiful and she was skilful at catching them.

But there was the problem—she could catch them, but she just couldn't eat them! It wasn't the smell, it wasn't the taste. Somehow, she just couldn't swallow them. Now, a seagull that can't eat fish is one very unhappy bird.

In the summertime it wasn't so bad. The little seaside town was full of holidaymakers who bought fast food as if they were starving, and carelessly dropped the remains. Susie lived on a diet of cheese sandwiches, sugary doughnuts and greasy chips. Of course, all this cholesterol was not good for her health or her figure. By August Bank Holiday Susie could barely fly back to her home at the end of the pier. In fact, she often took the train. Her brothers teased her unmercifully, calling her "Fatty" and "Blob" and other names too crude to mention here.

However, when September came, the holidaymakers went home and Susie, who relied on people for her survival, rapidly lost her excess weight. The residents of the little town didn't waste their food; their few scraps were binned, and the lids jammed down tight. Susie grew thinner and thinner, weaker and weaker; but she still couldn't stomach the fish her brothers caught for her.

Her mother did her best to tempt her, her father shouted at her, but all to no avail. Susie wouldn't, couldn't eat fresh fish.

Just before Christmas, Auntie Morag flew down from Scotland for a surprise visit. However, it was Auntie Morag who had the surprise, when she saw Susie.

"Why, hen, what have you been doing to yourself? You've lost the sheen on your feathers and you're so thin. You've never gone and developed that there anorexia, have you, child?"

Tearfully, Susie explained her problem.

Auntie Morag scratched her head. "I'll have to think about this. We can't let you just fade away. There must be an answer."

The matter wasn't mentioned again during the next few days. Each morning Auntie Morag would go for a long fly all by herself. She wouldn't say where she went, merely smiled and said they were reconnaissance flights.

A week later she came home with a lump of some grey-brown food in her beak. "Try this, Susie. See if you like it."

Watched anxiously by all the family, Susie tentatively nibbled the tiniest morsel. Everyone cheered when, not only did she swallow it, but opened her bill for more. Auntie Morag would not explain what the food was, or where it had come from. Each day, she fed Susie the new food. Susie grew stronger, and began taking short flights on her own. She even caught some fish for her brothers.

"It's time now for you to learn to feed yourself, for I must go back home to my own family. Be up early tomorrow, Susie, for we need to fly some way."

The next morning Susie was up and washed early, ready to discover the secret of the new food.

"First," said Auntie Morag, "you must catch a nice juicy fish."

"But I can't eat fish," wailed Susie.

"Dinna fash yourself, child. All will be revealed, soon."

Obediently, Susie neatly caught her fish.

"I'll carry it for you, hen, for we've a long flight and you don't have all your strength back yet."

Side by side they flew and flew. At last they came to a large kind of park with lawns and flowerbeds filled with berried shrubs, bare silver birches, bristly pines and a spreading cedar tree. A wide pathway led across the largest lawn to a churchlike building. In front of the building was a patio covered in beautiful flowers.

"Is this it, Auntie? Is this lovely place where you find my food?"

Auntie Morag nodded and then flew behind the building towards a tall chimney, covered with a metal grid. Aunt Morag laid her fish on the grid.

"Tomorrow," she explained, "your fish will be smoked and ready to eat."

"You mean that new food was fish. But I don't understand…"

"Susie, it was fresh fish you couldn't eat, smoked is just fine."

Susie was so excited she didn't notice the procession of shiny black cars slowly approaching the building.

"Auntie, Auntie, I won't have to rely on people ever again."

"Well," muttered Auntie Morag wryly, "not live ones, anyway!"

AMONGST THE PINE CONES

Mike Hemstock

Amongst the pine cones on the ground
A snowflake falls without a sound,
Followed by many more in a flurry.
See the animals, how they scurry.

The robin sings his wintry song,
And other warblers sing along.
He puffs his chest out, feeling merry,
Blending in with the holly berry.

The squirrels have their nuts in store,
They scamper about, looking for more.
Mistletoe berries sparkle white,
As the daylight turns to night.

Jack Frost's lurking; it's turning cold,
Affecting the young as well as the old.
He's working now, into the night,
Weaving his patterns. Oh, what a sight!

The fields around are covered in snow,
Rabbits nestle in their burrow.
Everything there is quite serene,
As I survey this wintry scene.

SONNET 3

Alfred J Holt

There is a haunting phantom, gaunt regret,
Whose bony hand rests chilly on our brow.
She yields no mercy, and once having met,
Her shadow trails us everywhere we go.

No heart would seek her out if known before,
She grips our soul and drags us, weeping hither,
Down the unlit, unending corridor,
Where yearning, our sad spirits fail and wither.

She led me, broken, to dark Hades' gate,
And said, "Come, enter" but I turned away,
Threw off the phantom, mastering my fate,
Resolved no more to wallow in lost days.

New strength have I for heights I hope to climb;
No more in thrall to ghosts long lost in time.

THE JOURNEY

Ann Cooper

The coach drove off. I sat in quiet contemplation
as the pale sun hovered over the morning mist;
Around me the comforting chatter of musical voices,
eagerly composing their own libretto.

"Wonderful voice but he sure should diet."
"Roaring drunk, near started a riot."
"Doctor told him he'd got nothing to fear."
"Took our summer holiday late last year."

The voices flowed in the air as I gazed
at Summer's green, dissolving into molten copper;
Ruby and jet stringing the hedgerows;
Distant woodlands haloed in sunlit amber glow.

"So I bought the gold one, thought it best."
"Brainy, our Brian, 'A' in his science test."
"Gift of the gab, she can tie him in knots."
"Headache, runny nose and covered in spots."

Grass verges measled with mole-hills;
Fairy dance of leaf shadows; streaking red fur;
Sorrowful flight of a lone magpie;
Milk-heavy cows queue at the gate.

"Guzzled champagne, went straight to her head."
"Fancies him rotten, wants him in bed."
"Sam drives that old car as if it's a tank."
"Hang on to him, he's got loads in the bank."

Silver birch hung with goblin gold;
Tossing head, bannered tail of a galloping stallion;
Refugee gulls circling brown, ploughed waves;
Lazy river idly drifting down to the sea.

The ladies were content with their conversation
and I was lost in my silent observation;
But now we've reached the final picture,
I wonder…whose experience was richer?

KATY-KOO

Shirley McIntyre

"Katy, how long has this been going on?" My treacherous tic should have warned her. "Well?"

"I'm sorry you found out like this. I was going to tell you, honestly. It was so hard finding the right moment, Davy."

"Oh, you poor darling. Now, let's see if I can help. When *would* be a good time to tell me you're shagging my best mate? Hmm, it is a tricky one, I agree. Let's think. Over a bottle of Moet, perhaps? Or between courses at Jamie's? No, no, no, silly me. Silly, silly dopey Davy-Dums. After the cruise, of course! You'd never jeopardise that would you, Katy-Koo?"

"Davy, please understand, we didn't mean to fall in love. It just happened."

"You trollop. Love? Ha! If you think Quentin Crumplebotham is capable of loving anyone but himself, you're even dumber than I thought. Quent's only emotion is in his trousers. He wanted to get his leg over, and you, silly cow, fell for it. Anyone would have done."

"It isn't like that. We're in love."

I wipe away the foamy spittle that tickles each side of my mouth. That barely discernible tic is now a full-blown twitch. My eyeballs pulse in a thick, red, mist. "Over my dead body, bitch."

Grabbing a knife I slash. Blood pumps. Screams become gurgles.

"Oh, my God, Katy, what have I done?"

Ramming a tea towel into the gaping gash, I drop the knife.

The gurgles stop.

The towel turns crimson. The love of my life is dead.

WITH YOUR HELP, JEREMY

Ann Cooper

Washing up and housework can wait for a while,
Time for my morning fix of Jeremy Kyle,
When the sad and the bad and the mildly insane
Eagerly seize their five minutes of fame.
"He treats me bad but no-one will listen."
"Is my little girl his'n or his'n?"

"She's cheated on me again and again."
"He's paranoid because of cocaine."
"My son's girlfriend is a dirty whore."
"I just can't take his abuse anymore."
"She's stinking drunk from morning till night."
"And life with him is absolute shite."

A single mum begs support for her child.
The out-of-work dad prefers to run wild.
A teenage father moans, "What can I do?
She's pregnant again. We've already got two!"
And Jeremy goes into one of his rants,
"Why don't you fellas keep it zipped in your pants?"

They all leave the stage, still full of stress,
And Graham is left to sort out the mess,
With friendly advice or a rehab clinic.
Now maybe it's cos I'm old, or maybe a cynic,
But if the world all around them is so full of strife,
Why don't they leave it behind them and go get a life.

WHISPER

Barrie J Kinsella

There it is again,
A sigh, a whisper,
Issuing from the forest glade,
With its patterned sunlight,
Set among the crowded tree surround,
Directed, it seems,
At my solitary figure.
I strain to hear
Its ongoing message.
Contentment flows over me
As understanding reveals
The answer to all problems,
As I stand in that forest glade,
Enwrapped in sunlight,
The mortal earth understood,
In the space of time, the heavens too,
The lengthening shadows
Adding a frame to the scene
Before me, as I raise my head
To seek out the dying rays
Of the setting sun
Before closure is brought
By eternal night.

GINGER AND BLACK

Dianne Rasmussen

"I have to have another cat," Judy said as she started clearing the table after breakfast.

John looked at her with a questioning expression.

"The pain of losing a pet is so horrendous, and the house seems so empty since we..." Judy's voice trembled as she continued, "lost...since Purdie died. Our house doesn't seem like our home without a cat."

After a minute or so John said, "Okay, if you're sure. But where are you going to find one?"

Judy smiled gratefully at him. He had been as upset as she when they had lost their intelligent tortoiseshell, and had said, "No more, we can't go through this again."

"Well, I thought I would ask Annie at the pet shop. She sometimes tries to find homes for kittens and cats that have lost their...." She paused before adding, "What should I call them? We never own a cat, so we are not owners, and 'carers' sounds as if they are not capable of looking after themselves, which most of them definitely are."

John laughed. "You could call yourself a voluntary slave, or just cat lover."

"Mmmm," she replied. "Anyway, I'll go and ask her today."

Later that morning, Judy went into the small shop in Northwood where she used to buy her cat food. She still returned occasionally to talk to Annie who worked there. After the usual introductory chit chat Judy, trying to keep the excitement out of her voice asked, "Do you know of any young cats who need a home?"

Annie did not look surprised, but smiled and said, "I wondered how long you'd last. It is for you?"

"Yes," Judy laughed. ""'m lonely without a cat, and I thought there may be some young ones who might need a home—adults rather than kittens because they are often more difficult to rehouse. Everyone loves kittens, but I love cats even more."

Annie smiled, picked up a pen and reached for her notebook. "Let's have your full name and telephone number." She wrote these down and then asked, "What sort do you want?"

Judy laughed and said, "Well, a cat is a cat, but I've always thought a black one and a ginger one would look stunning together, and I've never had a ginger one."

"I understand," said Annie. "Black and ginger would be nice, but if the cats need a home, you'll waive the colour?"

"Precisely." Judy then bought some cat food to put in the Cats' Protection box by the door.

The next day Judy received a telephone call from Annie: "Hello, Judy, I thought you'd be surprised to hear from me so quickly, but a lady came into our Montoe shop this morning and she has just what you're looking for. She's had two kittens for just over a month, and the lady she lives with turns out to be allergic to pet hairs, so she wants a really good home for them."

Judy gasped. She had not really expected to hear so soon, and was suddenly not sure she was ready. She didn't like to ask what colour they were, but grabbed a pen when Annie gave her the address and phone number.

It took only a few minutes for her uncertain feelings to give way to sympathy for the lady who had to find new homes for these kittens, and she phoned the number. A lady with a friendly voice and a slight Welsh accent answered. She questioned Judy about where she lived and what kind of a home she could give the young cats, and then said, “It sounds as if you’ll give them a safe and loving home. Can you come over now?”

Judy went to the house and came back with a long-haired black and white boy, called Boswell and a tabby girl, called Tigger 2. Their names were quickly shortened to Bozzie and Tiggie and Judy grew to love them even though they were not completely black or ginger.

Ten years later, John, Judy, Bozzie and Tiggie moved from their countryside home to the small neighbouring town. Their new home had a big garden but there were quite a few other houses nearby.

“It’s amazing to see so many cats around,” Judy said to her friend Tessa on the phone. “There’s even a ginger cat who lives in the garden that backs onto ours. He’s a friendly boy and is probably the nearest I'll ever get to having a ginger one.”

Six months later, she told Tessa, “There’s a very thin black cat who visits the garden and I’ve had to start feeding it.”

“Be careful,” warned Tessa. “Once it knows it can get food from you it’ll keep coming.”

And it did. It became quite friendly and began to put on weight. “Winter’s coming and I can't leave it out in the cold. Bozzie and Tiggie won’t like it, but they’ve stopped hissing at him, and I’m sure they’ll accept him eventually. I’ve decided to call him Prince after the Black Prince. I’m also going to have it neutered.”

The following week Judy told Tessa, “It seems that Prince is Princess and will be producing young any time now. Do you know anyone who wants a kitten?”

“Well, it's funny you should mention it, because I’ve just decided I would like a couple of kittens. Let me know when they’re ready and I’ll come to see them.”

Ten weeks later Tessa came and picked up two beautiful kittens, one black and one ginger.

COMPENSATION

Mike Hemstock

My burglar, he is suing me.
It's common, now I hear.
He came to pinch my valuables
One fateful night last year.

I heard him in the kitchen,
Searching every drawer,
Then as he grabbed my silverware,
I charged in through the door.

"Got you bang to rights," I cried,
Then seized him by the arm,
And this, the culprit later claimed,
'Had caused him lasting harm.'

It had made his heart beat faster,
And given him such a fright,
He'd had to give up burglary,
And going out at night.

He couldn't make a living,
Unless he got a job,
But, who'd employ a heartless man,
Whose talent was to rob?

I hear the 'Inland Revenue'
Had hired him right away,
And now he's suing me, because,
He gets a lot less pay.

The copper who arrested me,
He charged me with assault,
Agreed it was a pity,
But thought it was my fault.

He said, “In future, stay in bed,
And save yourself some grief,
Because, all the legal rights today,
Have been handed to the thief.”

A VALENTINE'S TREAT

Chrissie Lloyd

After forty years of marriage, Reginald and Norma were devoted to each other. Well. Reginald was devoted to Norma…most of the time.

"How are you, today, my love?" He gave her a concerned look.

"Bearing up, thanks, pet," she replied weakly, followed by a series of sniffles and twitching shoulder movements.

Norma was always 'bearing up' over some ailment. She liked reading medical books and appeared to acquire the illnesses she read about. Fortunately, her doctor would treat her—strangely with the same white, minty tablets—and restore her momentarily to good health.

Reginald neither questioned nor judged, just acted as a dutiful husband; would cook and wait on her, listen to her 'pain', knowing she could still eat and talk with enthusiasm.

The following day would be Valentine's Day.

In past years Reginald had surprised his beloved with interesting and romantic events. He had taken her wine-tasting in Calais, and travelled on the Orient Express. They had sleuthed at murder-mysteries, relaxed at health spas and 'wined and dined' at expensive restaurants. She had not enjoyed the paint-balling day, but had had a fabulous time at several zoos, theme parks, theatres, cinemas, and eaten more than her fair share of chocolate and ice cream.

Reginald racked his brain. *What shall we do this year? She likes eating, and boating—there are boats to hire on the lake at the local park. We could have a picnic. If we can't come up with any other brainwaves, that's what we'll do, if it's a nice day.*

It being a sunny Sunday, Reginald put on his best navy suit and polished his shoes until he could see his face in them. Norma had bought herself an expensive scarlet mohair dress and red, silk scarf.

At eleven o'clock they were ready for a good day out. He had prepared an elaborate hamper full of his wife's favourite things: dainty sandwiches with their crusts cut off, filled with salmon and cucumber, or beef or ham; individual pork pies; several packets of assorted flavoured crisps; and buttered teacakes. Then, as she had a sweet tooth, but was in her third year of being on a 'see food and eat it' diet, he placed, in the bottom of the hamper, a small chocolate gateau and a very large box of chocolates with less-fattening centres. Lastly, he carefully added a bottle of champagne.

Into her handbag Norma placed a red, heart-shaped valentine card for Reginald, on which she had carefully drawn five big kisses, and written 'Love from your devoted wife'.

They sat on the number sixteen city bus, food hamper sitting proudly in the luggage rack, pondering on past memories of their lives together, he, thinking himself the perfect husband, and she, wondering what had happened to her college sweetheart, Roger Blakely, who had bought a shiny, red sports car two weeks after they had split up.

The hamper had been a romantic idea but, once they had left the bus, it seemed to become heavier and heavier to Norma after she begrudgingly took hold of one of the handles. It required an epic manoeuvre, getting it aboard the boat. Its weight, combined with her fifteen stone, and Reginald's twelve stone caused the wooden craft to creak complainingly.

Once all three had taken their positions, Reginald rowing, hamper centre-stage, and Norma proud as a queen, enjoying the view, the grand journey commenced. She felt the warm breeze in her hair, he felt the beads of sweat trickle down his face. He wasn't as young or as fit as he used to be. He paused for a moment and let the boat float towards the water's edge until the foliage of an overhanging weeping willow tree tickled his back.

A two-year old boy in pale-blue shorts and white t-shirt stood nearby, gazing into the grey lake. "Water, water, water…" He jumped with glee on unsteady brown, chubby legs when he saw them.

"Where's your mum?" Reginald asked, fearing the child was too close to the edge.

Ignoring the question, the lad waved. "Me come with you?"

"Silly boy," Norma grumbled, munching on cheese and onion crisps. "Go back to your mum."

"Want a ride in boat." The boy stamped his feet.

A long-legged, sandy-coloured labrador bounded towards the toddler, wagging his tail and barking at the boat. The tail unbalanced the child, knocking him backwards, and he began to scream.

"Good gracious," Norma tried to shout above the screams. "Reginald, start rowing."

He held his breath, imagining what might have happened if the boy had fallen forwards into the cold water.

A young woman with long, auburn hair, and wearing faded blue jeans with holes in the knees, scooped the boy up and dragged him away from the lake while he pleaded, "I want a ride."

The labrador ran off in the opposite direction as Reginald took up the oars once again, dreaming of the day when his thirty-eight year old daughter would marry and give them grandchildren. He steered the boat away from the pathway, towards the centre of the lake.

The cries of the mother and toddler becoming more distant, two brave ducklings decided to waddle close to where Norma was eating her salmon sandwiches.

"Go away," she called, throwing pieces of bread out as far as she could in a bid to be rid of them. She couldn't abide birds, for they might have diseases they could pass on to her. Instead of them going, others joined them. The more food she threw, the more ducks appeared around them. Reginald was finding it difficult to row.

The breeze began to get cooler and the sky darkened. A large spot of rain dripped onto Norma's face. "Hey, watch what you're doing with those oars," she complained.

"Now what?" Reginald paused midstream of his tuneless rendition of 'Do You Think I'm Sexy'.

"You're splashing."

"Not me, love."

Then a flash of lightning lit up the sky, and more drops of rain began to fall.

"Reginald, I'm scared," she shrieked, clinging to the side of the boat, shooing away the ducks rushing for her fingers, hoping for more food.

They wandered off to find a new donator as the rain turned into hail stones, lashing down on them from all directions. "Take us back," she screamed, trying to wrap the scarf around her head but, her hands wet and cold, the red, silk accessory blew from her grasp. "What a wonderful Valentine's Day this is turning out to be."

As the small boat reached its destination, the rain stopped and the sun came out. The storm had lasted about five minutes, but the couple and their hamper were soaked. Norma sat in a pool of water, clinging to half a bottle of champagne. “I wish I’d put my wellies on,” she moaned, emptying water from her new, red shoes.

The boatman pulled the sodden couple from the boat. “What about your hamper?” he called after them, Norma still clutching the champagne, her dress dripping wet, and inches longer than when she had arrived.

“If you can find anything worth eating, you’re welcome to it,” Reginald shouted back.

The couple trudged to the bus stop, neither inspired to conversation, Reginald accepting to drink the last dregs of the champagne before throwing the bottle into a litter bin.

A few days later, Reginald became ill for the first time in five years, and had to take time off work with a bad dose of the flu. Norma became concerned for his health, but her pride and temperament would not allow her to forgive him for the disastrous day out. Her mohair dress had been ruined, along with her dignity. The red, expensive scarf had been lost. If she had gone back to the boating lake she would have seen the moorhen had woven it into the nest for her chicks.

ONE NIGHT STAND

Tony Butler

Sleep on, my love, and do not wake.
I will leave unseen.
Please let me carry, for awhile,
this foolish old man's dream.

One long night of tenderness,
enfolded and entwined;
your sweet flesh against my own,
and I have lost my mind.

I love you, oh, how stupid,
because I know, you see,
that you are but nineteen,
thirty-years too young for me.

Vulnerability forged the key,
you, sad, I, lonely.
It awakened feelings and emotions,
set them free.

Oh, how I really want to shake you,
wake you, take you.
False dreams I have of you.
Self delusion? Yes, it's true.

Transformed by your passion
into a young man once more,
I cannot face the journey back
through that old-man door.

I fear that should you wake
and I looked into your eyes,
I would see the reflections
of an old fool you'd despise.

It was I, you would think,
not your sadness and the drink,
that made you cross the threshold
at inhibition's brink.

You'd wish that our making love
last night had never been.
So sleep on, my love, and do not wake.
Let me leave unseen.

OUR JOURNEY

Alfred J Holt

Our journey started in our prime,
We listened to the church bells chime,
With promise of a lovely life,
'Twas then I took you for my wife.
It was amidst those August days,
So happy in our joyful ways,
Also blessed with golden weather,
We knew we would grow old together.

Under the stars of moonlit nights,
Embracing in our own delights,
When we were free of things to do,
I was so glad I married you.
We journeyed along life's bumpy roads,
And had to carry many loads,
Together always finding ways
To help us through the problem days.

We travelled on, just me and you,
'Til we were blessed with another two.
Years passed before they flew the nest;
Time then, my love, to have a rest.
But time it told, as nature intends,
The body unable to make amends,
Alas, arrived that dreadful day,
When you, my wife, did slip away.

By then I was well past my prime,
Alone to hear the church bell chime,
With journey's ending of our life,
I'm glad I took you for my wife.

POOR FELLOW

Mike Hemstock

The top that she wore on the night that she drowned,
A silky white blouse, and her skirt touched the ground.
She was due to be married the following morn.
The gown she would wear is still hanging forlorn.

It appears, on that night, she had gone for a walk
With a former boyfriend, to have a good talk.
There were bridges to cross, and roadways to build.
His passion was high, while she remained chilled.

As she ran along the towpath to get away from him,
Not seeing holes in the ground, she slipped and fell in.
She was screaming and shouting. "Help! I can't swim."
He called, "Where are you?" but the light was too dim.

She splashed and she gurgled for a very long while,
And, when all went quiet, he ran for a mile.
He felt really guilty for what he had done.
He couldn't tell anyone, not even his mum.

Her fiancé, unknowing what deed had been done,
Came home from his stag night. He'd had so much fun.
He dressed in his new shirt, the following day.
Their passports were ready. They were going away.

When told of the mishap, he sat down and cried.
Never again would he see his beautiful bride.
He remained a recluse for the rest of his life,
Thinking of his tragically-drowned, would-be wife.

ILL WIND

Nell

North pulled down the corner of his eye and examined it in the mirror. No doubt about it, he didn't feel his normal self. His eyes were gritty, he had a prickling sensation in his nose, and his throat felt dry; what a time to go down with a cold, with his busiest month coming up.

He shouted down to his wife who he could hear rattling around the kitchen. 'Do you have any of those hot lemon jobs? I'm coming down with the 'flu.'

The rattling stopped. North heard an exaggerated sigh, a mutter which sounded suspiciously like "Man 'Flu", then the "click" of the kettle being switched on. A couple of minutes later his wife, Southerly, came up with a steaming mug.

'You only have a bit of a cold. Drink this and get a wiggle on!'

North sipped tentatively at the mug; as he thought, too hot. That was the trouble with being married to a southerner, always wanting too much heat. He left it on the side to cool, and carried on dressing. He had a busy day ahead; mind you, they were all busy at that moment. He had been rostered to work with that new Easterly; fancy getting someone in from abroad—all the way from the Urals, they said. His hot lemon cooled, he even finished the powdery bits in the bottom.

Feeling slightly better, he hurried off to work. He was just warming up with a nice force three over Scotland when the sneezing started. Oh, damn, he'd gusted up to gale force with that one and he wasn't down to reach Northern England until lunch time; at that rate he'd be in Derby by mid-morning.

He felt a chilly blast to his left and saw the new chap approaching.

'Dobraeh utrah, Comrade. Vot a gust! A man on the hills vas blown over!'

North looked down; without a doubt East had increased the chill factor. All around the North of England people were pulling on hats, and fishing in pockets for gloves. East was one of those who enjoyed getting one over the weather forecasters.

'Almost as good as your vife ven she caught Michael Fisch napping.'

North gritted his teeth. Would anybody ever forget his wife's hurricane back in 1987? A sneeze caught him unawares and he watched as a high-sided vehicle teetered for a moment, then settled back on its wheels.

East clapped his hands in glee and joined in. North just didn't feel up to stopping him. He could see East busy herding a bank of cloud and, when he looked back, a blanket of white was settling over the Grampians. Oh, well, might as well let them have a white Christmas. He whipped up some cumulo nimbus over the sea and ushered them into Cumbria. Very soon the fells were looking festive.

A couple of sneezes later, North began to enjoy himself. He hadn't caused so much mischief since his teens, and East was really going for it. Together they got behind an Arctic High, which had been hovering around Norway, and forced it southwards. The weak Low, which had been dominating the Southern half of England, was no match for a pressure system born and bred in the high North; they soon had it cleared out of the way. They stopped for lunch while more cloud had a chance to form over Europe.

Over coffee and sandwiches, East mentioned he'd only just been promoted to Major Wind, which explained his eagerness. North told him about his children; all had left home. Chinook was working in North America and his younger brother, Zonda, in Argentina. The girls, Mistral and Sirrocco were both in the Med.

By then North's throat felt really sore and his voice had begun to disappear.

East looked at him sympathetically, but with a hint of calculation. Easterlies had always varied between mischievous and downright evil.

'Tell you vot, you just keep that Low out of the vay, and I'll deal with the Arctic system and cloud cover.'

Feeling rough, North didn't care anymore. He just nodded and let East carry on. Besides, if he was serious about handling both, there'd be overtime involved, and he'd promised to be home on the dot. He moved over a little and kept up a steady blow against the hapless low; it really was a weak affair with only a little light rain on its leading edge. His nose had started to block up, and the occasional sneeze would send an icy blast through Wales.

East was thoroughly enjoying himself. By late afternoon, he'd allowed enough clear sky to provide a good frost and, by early evening, he had marshalled his initial shower clouds. The Low Pressure system snivelled some drizzle over the Channel Islands, and trundled off to try its luck over Normandy. North waved goodbye to East.

'Dasvidaniya, Comrade,' shouted East, and set about pushing some heavy snow showers off the North Sea into Yorkshire.

North headed home. The Wests would be coming for dinner, and he didn't feel like it one bit; all he wanted was an early night.

He manfully resisted the urge to call in for a swift drink, and was rewarded by the look of surprise on his wife's face as he walked in exactly on time. He sniffed the air; no smell of cooking and the table hadn't been laid.

'What's up?' he queried. 'Aren't the Wests coming?'

'No. He's run off with Hurricane Delilah from Jamaica. She was in such a state when she 'phoned I could hardly hear, but I gather he's been posted to the Pacific, and she's currently causing floods in Spain and Portugal.' Southerly started to grin, then a giggle escaped. 'I never knew he had it in him! I've been on the 'phone all afternoon; it's the talk of the entire weather system. Be a love and nip to the Indian. Mine's a Chicken Balti.'

North headed back out, smiling to himself. Fancy boring old West going off with a Hurricane; it'd make old Sou'wester's year.

He'd have to nip into the pub while he waited for the curry.

The following morning, North's cold had arrived in earnest, together with a tight chest and a hacking cough. Southerly packed him a flask of hot soup, a supply of pills and cough mixture and, reluctantly, he headed off to work. He looked down in amazement at East's overnight efforts; almost the whole of Britain was covered with snow, even a sprinkling on Land's End, and it was always difficult to make it stick there. Gritters were stuck at odd angles, with lines of traffic backed up behind them and everywhere he looked the rush hour was in chaos. That was the thing about England, giving them a bit of snow to cope with was so rewarding.

East was busy over the North Sea. He looked shattered and merely flapped a hand in greeting.

‘Very good snow, East,’ commented North. ‘You look a bit short on cloud cover, would you like some from the North Atlantic?’

‘That vould be great. The veather over Europe is vorn out and von’t make cloud fast enough.’

North ambled off towards Greenland. One could always find a good supply of cloud there. He gathered plenty into a solid mass, so full of snow, it made pushing it down into Cumbria tough going.

North sniffed, tried to clear the tickle from his throat with a dose of Old Twistleton’s Patent Cough Cure, and blew as hard as he could. The cloud, sensing action ahead, cooperated and very soon the fells had received a second coat of the white stuff.

Once it began, there was no stopping it. On it went, producing blizzards at first, with a steady fall following behind. Lancashire and Yorkshire received their share and then on it went, down into the Midlands. By lunch time it was causing chaos on the North Circular and made headlines on the news. North and East sat back, shared North’s soup and watched it.

East yawned and stretched. North could see he was exhausted. ‘Tell you what, you pop off and get some kip. I’ll keep the front in place and we’ll let them have a clear night with plenty of frost. That’ll give them time to clear the main roads so they can get about a bit and enjoy a white Christmas.’

Too new and keen, East didn’t look happy at that. ‘You’re just a big softie at heart,’ he grumbled. ‘I’m too vacked to argue. See you after Christmas.’ He ambled off back to the Urals.

North took a couple of pills and a giant swig of cough mixture and, blowing gently, he forced the clouds over the South coast just in time for dusk to settle.

One by one the stars started to twinkle and the temperature plummeted.

North walked home, watching the moon peep above the horizon, frost halo firmly in place. Down below, carol singers gathered and warmly-wrapped up children ran round throwing snowballs.

North grinned. He knew most adults hated the weather, but somehow the crisp whiteness gave an extra zest to the singing, and reminded them all of Christmas past. Perhaps being an ill wind wasn't so bad after all.

A LIFE NOT LIVED

Alfred J Holt

Is our only life foretold and writ
In Heaven's book?
Are we yoked as blindfold oxen,
Treading to the master's whim?
If, somehow, we backwards see
What might and might not be,
Could we then be free of him?
I think not, what's done is done,
Foreordained, as blind men shuffle,
With guiding hand on shoulder,
Kindness fleeting, but not for all;
Perhaps for some who love life,
And for whom life loves back;
For others just the lonely road
To blessed oblivion's silent hall.
Some welcome death's slow tread
Upon the stair,
Their face alights with joy
When life departs.
Cowardly or bold, it matters not.
When shutters softly close at last,
Who cares?

A BABY CALLED HOPE

Angela Rigley

I'll never forget her beautiful eyes,
their colour as blue as the sky
in summer,
or cornflowers in the meadow.
They seemed to look through you;
though unseeing was she,
my blind baby girl,
who sadly now lies
so lifeless and still
in her new resting place.
No more cries will I hear,
or sighs of distress.
Never again will I see
her sweet little face,
which I once
held so dear.
But I know
she is up there,
enjoying the bliss
of heavenly rapture,
with God,
who has called
my Hope
to be his.

AUTHOR BIOGRAPHIES

David Brailsford

I was born in Nottingham in 1930, and educated at the High Pavement Grammar School. I worked as a Senior Nursing Officer, developing a Staff in-house Training Department. Now retired, I spend my time writing and telling stories. My Jamaican-born wife is my inspiration for my books about Jamaica: 'Duppy Stories', 'Confessions of Anansi', 'Jamaican Witchcraft', and I have also written a book about my experiences when working in Mental Health, now on Amazon Kindle. I have three daughters and many grand and great grandchildren. Details of my work can be seen on the following websites: www.lmhpublishingjamaica.com and www.amazon.com

Gordon F Butler

I am a retired teacher who has three main interests in life: my family, my photography and my writing, along with a continued love of everything 'railways'. I began writing after retiring in 1996 when I joined Eastwood Writers' Group. Later I contacted Radio Nottingham and after submitting a trial piece, I have been recording my own 'Thoughts for the Day' and 'Sunday Reflections'. So far the number written and recorded runs at almost two hundred and I am still writing them.

Tony Butler

I was born in 1942 and live in Derbyshire with my wife, Sue. A professional magician since 1970, I began writing routines and patter for other magicians and also one-line gags for comedians. My published novels are: 'Merlin's Granddaughter' for children 11-13; 'Different' a science fiction novel for young adults; and 'Killing Kat' an adult thriller.

Ann Cooper
I am a retired primary schoolteacher now enjoying my life (and second childhood!) making cards, singing in a choir and, of course, writing.

Mike Hemstock
I have four grandchildren between the ages of eight and fourteen. They are my pride and joy. I was a bricklayer before retiring in September 2000. I wrote my first poem in 1975 entitled 'Ode to a Referee'. It was based on the experiences I had whilst refereeing football matches. It was twenty nine years later when I started writing again, in 2003, when I joined Eastwood Writers' Group. I have written many poems, and have included some in a booklet that I self published. You can see a cross section of them in this anthology.

Alfred J Holt
I was born and raised in South London and now live in Pinxton. I retired five years ago. For the last twenty-four years I trained and worked as a chef. I started writing four years ago, and tend to write romantic poetry and light-hearted short stories. I have been published in some local newspapers and magazines.

Annette Jones
I used to study medieval Norway, but had to give up due to ill health; I have had arthritis since I was twenty. I don't recommend it. Arthritis, that is, not medieval Norway. At least I now have more time to write fiction and work on finishing a novel. I get closer every year,

especially in November, as I participate in National Novel Writing Month. I sew, crochet and knit, like to dress up in medieval or Victorian clothes, and I time travel (do re-enactments) and play the bowed psaltery. I think that makes me sound quite interesting, but actually I don't get out much. You don't even have to get out of bed to write, which is one of my favourite things about it. My cat agrees, but my husband just hopes I will write a bestseller one day.

Barrie J Kinsella
I came to writing late, with the ambition to join and be one of the 'real writers'.

Chrissie Lloyd
I have enjoyed creative writing since an early age, have won a few writing competitions and had a short story in My Weekly. I have not published a novel yet, but keep enjoying trying. I live on my own, like a spot of gardening and the occasional holiday.

Shirley McIntyre
I was born and raised in The Meadows, Nottingham. I've been married to Rob for 43 years—eek, how did that happen! We have two lovely daughters and four wonderful granddaughters. I've always been a bit of a wordsmith but it's only been in recent years that I've had the time to focus on my writing. I'm proud to say that, with the help and encouragement from the members of Eastwood Writers' Group, Jacksdale Jotters, and Mike Wareham at the Tin Hat Centre, I now have a regular column in a local publication.

Nell
I am from the Midlands and work part-time as an Alter Ego. My job involves creating flights of fancy to distract my employer from the more boring aspects of the everyday world. At times I am all too successful, resulting in several instances of milk in the cupboard and tea in the fridge and, on one memorable occasion, gravy seasoned with sugar and custard with salt.

Dawn Raffle
I have always worked in the community in a caring environment. I spent many years working for a local authority as a Scheme Manager in Sheltered Housing; I have always loved reading and when I retired, I found the time to write stories of my own, for others to enjoy.

Dianne Rasmussen
I am a retired History Teacher who loves writing about anything, but particularly cats. I have been a member of Eastwood Writers' Group for eight years.

Angela Rigley
Married to Don, I have 5 children and 8 grandchildren, and was educated at Alton Convent in Hampshire. My books, all set in Victorian times, are 'Looking for Jamie', 'A Dilemma for Jamie', 'School for Jamie', 'Choices for Jamie' and 'Lea Croft' published by Bluewood Publishing. They can be purchased from there, or from Amazon. I have also written 2 other novels yet to be published. My hobbies include genealogy (having traced ancestors back to 1520); flower arranging; singing in my church choir; playing Scrabble and gardening. I've had several jobs doing accounts and, oh, I am also the Treasurer of Eastwood Writers' Group. My website is

www.nunkynoo.yolasite.com and my blog site is www.authoryantics.wordpress.com. I am on Facebook, LinkedIn, Goodreads and Twitter www.twitter.com/angie rigley,.

Harry Riley
Married with a grown up son and daughter, I was educated at John Player School and Nottingham college of Arts. I enjoy reading and writing short stories, novels and poetry, and am interested in history. My published mystery novels are: 'Sins of the Father' and 'The Laird of Castle Ballantine'; my short story collections: 'Captain Damnation and Other Strange Tales' and 'Wreckers and Other Strange Tales'; 'Terror, Tinsel and Turkey', a Christmas anthology, published by Pneuma Springs; and Pentrich Revolution short stories: 'Twisting In' and 'Butchered & Bled for a Loaf of Bread'. My YouTube videos: harryriley321 and harryxxxxxriley. I am on Facebook and my websites are: www.harryspen.co.uk, www.eastwoodchapterverse.yo#13BEF35, www.spanglefish.com/lifeariley
www.millsideradio.co.uk

Copyright attributions

Cover design by Annette Jones. Window picture by Annette Jones. Small images variously sourced.

Unattributed small images are public domain.

Six small images from within group:

"Cats Tiggy and Bozzy" by Dianne Rasmussen

"Dogs Dolly and BoBo" by Shirley McIntyre

"Lambs" and "Snowy Garden" by Angela Rigley

"Train" by Gordon Butler

"Black Horse" by Annette Jones

Six small images, cropped and resized, from the following Creative Commons sources:

"To The Sea We Went" by Faisal Akram CC BY-SA 2.0

http://commons.wikimedia.org/wiki/File:To_The_Sea_We_Went_(3961508567).jpg

"Utetheisa bella" Moth by Eddie McGriff, University of Georgia, Bugwood.org CC BY 3.0 US

http://commons.wikimedia.org/wiki/Category:Moths_of_the_United_States#mediaviewer/File:Utetheisa_bella.jpg

"Two covered pies (strawberry rhubarb) mostly finished" by Kellen CC BY-SA 3.0

http://commons.wikimedia.org/wiki/File:23-pies_finished.jpg

"Taraxacum, the plant" Dandelion by Arnoldius CC BY-SA 2.5

http://commons.wikimedia.org/wiki/File:Taraxacum_plant.jpg

"Chaldon Church" Graves by Allen Watkin CC BY-SA 2.0

http://commons.wikimedia.org/wiki/File:Graves_(671048651).jpg

"Red Fox at Ystad, Sweden" by Jonn Leffmann CC BY 3.0

http://en.wikipedia.org/wiki/Fox#mediaviewer/File:R%C3%A4v_vid_Revhusen_i_Ystad_-_Juli_2012..jpg

Two small images, cropped, from http://www.freeimages.com/ following their own license agreement found at http://www.freeimages.com/help/7_2 copyright belongs either to freeimages or to the image provider:

"Ink Well and Quill Pen" by Stephen J. Sullivan

http://www.freeimages.com/photo/558332

"Soccer ball and net" by Annette Crimmins

http://www.freeimages.com/photo/9997977

36101577R00138

Made in the USA
Charleston, SC
25 November 2014